# 14 KEYS
# TO
# LASTING
# LOVE

## ALSO BY KIM KIMBERLING

7 Secrets to an Awesome Marriage

7 Secrets to an Awesome Marriage Discussion Guide

Preparing for an Awesome Marriage

Preparing for an Awesome Marriage Student Workbook

The 30-Day Experiment for Singles

The 30-Day Experiment: Taking Your Marriage
to a Whole New Level

# 14 KEYS TO LASTING LOVE

## How to Have the Marriage You've Always Wanted

## KIM KIMBERLING, PhD

New York  Nashville

FaithWords
Hachette Book Group
1290 Avenue of the Americas, New York, NY 10104
faithwords.com
twitter.com/faithwords

First Edition: January 2019

FaithWords is a division of Hachette Book Group, Inc. The FaithWords name and logo are trademarks of Hachette Book Group, Inc.

The publisher is not responsible for websites (or their content) that are not owned by the publisher.

The Hachette Speakers Bureau provides a wide range of authors for speaking events. To find out more, go to www.hachettespeakersbureau.com or call (866) 376-6591.

Library of Congress Cataloging-in-Publication Data

Names: Kimberling, Kim, author.
Title: 14 keys to lasting love : how to have the marriage you've always
    wanted / Kim Kimberling, PhD.
Other titles: Fourteen keys to lasting love
Description: first [edition] | New York : Faith Words, 2019. | Includes
    bibliographical references.
Identifiers: LCCN 2018026344 | ISBN 9781546010067 (trade pbk.) | ISBN 9781549199844
    (audio download) | ISBN 9781546010074 (ebook)
Subjects: LCSH: Marriage—Religious aspects—Christianity.
Classification: LCC BV835 .K5426 2018 | DDC 248.8/44—dc23
LC record available at https://lccn.loc.gov/2018026344

ISBNs: 978-1-5460-1006-7 (paperback), 978-1-5460-1007-4 (ebook)

Printed in the United States of America

LSC-C

10 9 8 7 6 5 4 3 2 1

*This book is dedicated to my amazing grandkids—Sunny, Tag, Tommy, Gracie, and Eli. You each bring so much joy to my life and you inspire me to continue the fight for awesome marriages. I love you all.*

# PRAISE FOR *14 KEYS TO LASTING LOVE*

"I felt I was getting the amazing counseling, coaching, and insight from Dr. Kim Kimberling on every page of *14 Keys to Lasting Love*. This book is so very practical and hopeful. Kim is not only a wonderful counselor and leader with Awesome Marriage but has lived out what he writes about with his own marriage and now adult children."

—Jim Burns, PhD, president, HomeWord, author of *Creating an Intimate Marriage* and *Doing Life with Your Adult Children: Keep Your Mouth Shut and the Welcome Mat Out*

"Dr. Kim Kimberling has written an outstanding book for anyone interested in having a happy, successful marriage. His '14 Essential Keys' are proven fundamental building blocks to a great marriage. Written in a down-to-earth, enjoyable style, the wisdom in this book will truly help you to become a better spouse!"

—Rick Johnson, bestselling author of *Becoming Your Spouse's Better Half* and *Romancing Your Better Half*

"Weaving in stories from his counseling practice, Dr. Kimberling provides practical insight for navigating a broad range of issues that impact marriage, including several important ones you've likely not seen covered in a marriage book before! *14 Keys to Lasting Love* is a great read for any couple, regardless of length of marriage or season, and will serve as a marriage check-up and a conversation starter with your spouse."

—J. Parker, Christian intimacy author and speaker

"As a young bride, I sat on the sofa and cried. My real marriage was not like the movies. We were both Christians and believed God brought us together. I assumed his divine endorsement would make everything easy. But it didn't, and it wasn't. It was hard and not at all what I expected. I wish we had this book in our early years. It is filled with essential tools for building a relationship you can both enjoy. Instead of a throwing out a magical checklist, it empowers couples to explore, define, and determine to do the work that will make their unique marriage work. As Dr. Kimberling states, 'Nothing just works itself out in marriage.' Creating a vibrant life together takes effort, but any couple who grabs hold of these 14 keys will save time, energy, and tears."

—Lynn Marie Cherry, author of *Keep Walking: 40 Days to Hope and Freedom after Betrayal*

"Marriage can be hard! *14 Keys to Lasting Love* is a great tool for strong and weary couples alike. Dr. Kimberling addresses many problems marriages face today, and then provides the couple with practical steps to build and strengthen a marriage. I'm so thankful for this resource, and finished the book feeling encouraged, and empowered. I will be passing it along."

—Shauna N. Shanks, speaker and author of *A Fierce Love*

"Having known Dr. Kim Kimberling for years, I can tell you that there is no better person to write this book. Everything that Dr. Kim produces is packed with practical insights into how to have an awesome marriage, and this book is no different. Reading this book feels like you're in Dr. Kim's living room just soaking in the wisdom for your marriage from someone who has both lived it in his own marriage and spent his entire career bettering marriages."

—Nils Smith, author and chief strategist of social media and innovation at Dunham and Company

"If you're ready for real help toward building a loving marriage that lasts a lifetime, then *14 Keys to Lasting Love* is for you! In Dr. Kim's easy-to-read manner you'll learn how to: heal the broken areas of your marriage, reframe how you view your spouse, grow in commonality amidst raising kids and stresses of life, rekindle intimacy and sex in your marriage, and become the couple you always hoped you'd be."

—Rhonda Stoppe, No Regrets Woman, speaker, and author of *Real-Life Romance* and *The Marriage Mentor: Becoming the Couple You Long to Be*

"If you would like to take your relationship up a notch or two, this book may be just what you've been looking for. Based on a survey of married couples, Dr. Kim has identified the key areas where most couples struggle or at least want to improve. We were amazed by how practical and easy it is to apply the *14 Keys to Lasting Love*. You'll glean insights from Dr. Kim and from real-life stories. But it doesn't stop there! Each Key has tips for Going Deeper, to help you actually do what you have learned. Your relationship will definitely take a leap forward!"

—Claudia Arp and David Arp, MSW, authors of *10 Great Dates to Energize Your Marriage*

"*14 Keys to Lasting Love* is your handbook to practical ways of investing in and caring for your marriage. From your emotional health to your physical health, and everything in between, Dr. Kimberling offers you suggestions that will make you feel like the marriage you've always wanted isn't just possible—it's right around the corner."

—Debra Fileta, MA, LPC, author of *Choosing Marriage* and creator of TrueLoveDates.com

# CONTENTS

# INTRODUCTION

There are a lot of awesome markers in a wedding ceremony: the groom seeing his bride in her dress for the very first time when she glides down the aisle; the pastor pronouncing them "husband and wife"; the couple, all smiles, walking down the aisle hand in hand to begin their life together. As the couple slips into their "Just Married" car while being showered with rice, all their hopes and dreams lay bright before them. It's a great occasion. It's a time to celebrate. It's the precursor to "happy ever after."

Proverbs 18:22 says, "He who finds a wife finds what is good and receives favor from the Lord" (NIV). What a great promise! Yet one of the really tough things for me as a marriage counselor is looking at that couple and knowing statistically that they have a fifty-fifty chance of making it. That can feel gut-wrenching.

But as a marriage counselor, I also know that *every* couple can make it. Not just by surviving their marriage but by building a marriage that thrives. Every couple can have the marriage God designed specifically for them. What does it take? Time, effort, and commitment. And most important? Putting God in their individual lives and at the center of their marriage, where He *has* to be. And putting their spouse where God wants them to be. The time and effort and commitment are more than worth it.

We will look at 14 essential keys to help you have the marriage you always wanted. This is not a checklist. It is an opportunity to look deep into your marriage and together with your spouse build something step-by-step that you both will cherish. Depending on your life experiences and where you are in your marriage, some of the keys will present more challenges than others. But when you put them all together, you will have created a template of lasting love for you and your spouse.

As we journey through this book, my prayer for you is that you will be encouraged and have hope in what God will do in your marriage. You will meet a number of couples and hear their stories. Some will encourage you, and you will learn from their experiences. Others will sadden you as you see them heading for disaster. But this I know: your marriage will be better and you will be more in sync with God than you ever thought possible. It's time to begin. Let's get going!

# CHAPTER 1

# Staying on Track: Commonality and More

## COMMON INTERESTS

Nancy and I were a pretty typical couple when we were dating. We believed we were alike. We were aware that we had some differences, but they seemed insignificant. We were the perfect couple who had it all figured out. Our wedding was just the first step to our "happily ever after." The bubble didn't burst suddenly after the honeymoon. It was more like we let the air out a little at a time. I think we both realized as we began our second year of marriage that we had done a lot to appease each other while we dated and through our engagement. If I wanted to do something, Nancy was on board, and vice versa. We did have a lot of common interests, but we didn't have the same passion for all of them. For instance, I loved ice hockey and Nancy would willingly go to games with me. She even learned the rules and who the players were and took an interest in our local team. We shared a common interest, but this is where the difference came in: I wanted season tickets so we could go to every game. She thought that was a bad idea because there was no way we would go to every single game. Instead of agreeing with my idea that we go to all thirty-six home games, she thought eight or nine a season was a better fit for us. Common interest? Yes. Same game plan for pursuing it? No.

## MATT AND CHRISTINE

Matt and Christine had been married for five years and were searching for a certified marriage counselor when they made an appointment with me. They fell in love in college and continued to date as they both completed graduate school. The week after they walked the stage to accept their graduate diplomas, they walked the aisle in their church to become husband and wife. They took an abbreviated honeymoon because they were both starting new jobs. The plan was to take their extended honeymoon a year later at vacation time. That never happened.

Matt and Christine really cared for each other, and neither was trying to get out of the marriage. They just had very little connection, if any. From the day they met, their relationship was always second to school in the early years and to their careers in the later years. As we talked, they realized their common interest in college and grad school was studying and being at the top of the class. Not a bad thing, but they didn't take time to develop other interests together.

As they opened up to me, they remembered talking together in the first days of their marriage about things couples do together, things they hoped they could learn to enjoy together. Yet, as they got into their new jobs, they both worked more hours than they'd expected, and when they did have free time, it was easier to lounge around their apartment. That list of things they hoped to do was long gone and forgotten until we talked about it that first day in counseling.

Matt and Christine had a void in their marriage. They had no common interests. Their life consisted of work and church for an hour on Sunday (and they both worked from home on the weekends). That was about it for waking hours. This marriage was probably not headed for disaster. Rather it was two people existing side by side with no way of connecting. If nothing changed, they were going to spend a lifetime separately together.

In a situation like Matt and Christine's, there are some major decisions that need to be made if things are going to change. Many couples verbally express a desire for things to be different, but when it comes down to making changes, the consequences of change are more than they want to bear. Matt loved his job. He made really good money. He also worked a lot of hours each week. The same was true for Christine. As we talked, they could see that they had to initiate any changes. Nothing was going to change on its own. They batted around some ideas. They could both work fewer hours and keep their jobs, but they would make less money and probably miss out on the bonuses they had gotten used to. The truth was that if just one of them scaled back, it would not bring the change they needed.

What would you do in their situation? Plan A called for both to scale back work. That meant a monetary life change and maybe even downsizing to a smaller home. Yet it would free up time for them to pursue their marriage. Plan B was to stay status quo. Keep up the work pace. Make more money. Build a bigger house. Accept the fact that their marriage was about as good as it would get. Would you choose Plan A or Plan B?

## BEING BETTER

Janis and David had been married nine years. As they shared their story, they both used the same phrase when talking about each other: "You used to be such a good husband" and "You used to be such a good wife." It struck me: "used to be good." What happened? I looked at David and asked, "What was different for you when you were such a good husband?" He stared at me blankly as he gave my question some thought. His answer spoke volumes: "I used to ask myself almost every day, 'How can I be a better husband to Janis?' I guess I haven't asked myself that question in a very long time."

There was a time in their marriage when being a good husband and being a good wife were priorities. Janis answered my "what happened?" question almost the same way David did. I don't think David and Janis are in this boat alone. If most of us were honest with ourselves, I think we would say something similar.

How many couples hit the ground running trying to do everything they can to be the best husband and the best wife possible? I think most couples could say they start off this way. Then it seems most of us run into a wall. Some hit the wall pretty soon after marriage, while for others the hit comes down the line. Most of us will at one time or another during our marriage. The real problem is not with hitting the wall. It's what we will do afterward. David and Janis never got back on track. They quit asking the question. Their marriage, which started out so well, drifted into a so-so relationship. They never actually fought, but there was a big void that wasn't filled.

Asking yourself every day how you can be a better spouse is a terrific place to start. Asking yourself that question daily and also asking God to help you be a better spouse takes it to a whole new level. It will change your marriage. So you know what drives me crazy both in myself and in others? We find something that works and really makes a difference, and then we quit doing it!

When David and Janis quit asking themselves the question, it wasn't because they had a crisis in their marriage. Instead it was this: One day David didn't ask himself the question. That day the marriage was still good. Then the next day he forgot to ask, and slowly the days began to add up, day after day without asking "the question." This is what usually happens when we get into this pattern. We are not aware of the change in our marriage. We slip apart ever so slowly. We tell ourselves that we have it figured out, our marriage has arrived, and we can slow down. So over a period of time we end up just like David and Janis or Kim and Nancy or thousands of other couples. We start out with great intentions of doing the "right things" and asking the "right question." But we stop when things are good because we think we can coast the rest of our marriage. You know what Nancy and I learned? We cannot coast! Coasting and marriage do not go together. The time we need for working out what it is to be a good husband or a good wife can get filled quickly with something else, and that something else is usually not something bad. It becomes bad when it takes priority over our spouse.

My life and my marriage are better when I ask myself how I can be a good husband and then ask God for His help. God answers that prayer. I get to watch Him show me how much He cares about me and our marriage. There are days when I pray that prayer in the morning and then instead of being purposeful about following through with it, I let life get in the way. But you know what God does? He remembers for me. Sometime in the day I'll get a prompt that I know without a doubt is Him giving me a "good husband" idea. It may be to send a Bitmoji text to Nancy because she loves to get them. It may be doing the dishes after dinner to give Nancy a break. Since Nancy's love language is quality time, it may be setting aside extra time to be with her. God is always faithful to answer that prayer. Doesn't it make sense? He wants you to have an awesome marriage. He wants to answer your prayers that are for your good. Of course He is going to show up.

When was the last time you asked yourself how you could be a better spouse? Whether it was yesterday or so long ago that you cannot remember, why not make it a routine today? While you are at it, why not ask for God's help? Give our amazing God a chance today to shower you with His incredible love!

### HOW CAN I SUPPORT YOU?

I've listened to Andy Stanley's podcasts for a number of years, often early in the morning while I work out. I like his style, and he challenges me. I don't always like the challenges though! On this particular Monday morning, I was having a great workout. My run went well and I was pushing through the weights. It was an amazing start to a new day. Then Andy said this: "Ask your spouse how you can help them today." At first I thought, *That's a good idea. I know a couple I am counseling who could use that idea. It could really help their marriage.* It was about this time I realized that he was not talking to them. Andy was talking to *me.* So I thought, *That is a pretty good idea I can try sometime but not today. I am really busy. Yes, I will be at home working today, but I have writing to do, podcasts to record, and a lot of other things on my Monday to-do list.*

A couple of hours later that same morning, I was sitting at my desk in my study, listening to music with my earbuds in and writing. I was in my own world and totally enjoying it. For Nancy, Monday is wash day. She walked through my office from our bedroom with a full laundry basket. For some reason I looked up, saw her, and thought, *Andy did not mean for me to ask her that today.* A couple of minutes later, she walked back through, and I thought, *Yes, he did.* So I looked up from my laptop and said, "How can I help you today?" I must not have said that in a long time, if ever, because I got a blank stare back. A long blank stare that silently said, *Are you okay?* Finally, Nancy said, "I can't think of anything, but thanks for asking." I let out a quiet sigh of relief and thought, *That's great. I just made points by not doing anything. That Stanley guy is a genius!*

I wanted that to be one of those checklist things. You know: *I did it and now I can check it off and not worry about doing it again.* That's what I wanted, but that's not what God wanted. I felt a nudge telling me that this was a good idea and I needed to embrace it. As I thought back to Andy's podcast, I remembered what he really said: "*Every day* ask your spouse how you can help them." Every day!

So now that's what I try to do. You know what? It has made a difference in our marriage, and I don't get the blank stare anymore. Some days I get, "It would be great if you would…" and other days, "No, but I really appreciate you asking." You know what else? I like the difference it has made in me.

What about you? How about asking your spouse today? Sure, it may be awkward the first time. She or he may think you have completely lost it, but you will love the difference it makes in your marriage. Honestly, you really have nothing to lose, and I promise you, there is a lot to gain.

## CONNECTION

Nancy and I could fill a notebook with the list of things we have done wrong in our marriage over the years. Fortunately, we have done some things right too. One thing we feel has made a difference is the time each day that we set aside to check in with each other. There were years when it was harder to find that time, but almost without exception we found it. Some days it was five minutes, other days thirty minutes or more. Those "thirty minutes or more" days have always been my favorites.

Getting couples to set aside time each day to connect is usually a process. It's not that they say they don't want to or that they have something better to do. Usually the tough part is carving out time and holding it sacred when schedules scream for their focus to be elsewhere. Todd and Jessica had three kids, who were spaced the "perfect" two and a half years apart. Their oldest was ten, then seven plus, and five. My guess is that you can relate in one way or another to their lives. Jessica homeschooled the two youngest, and the oldest was in public school. Todd had a really good job that usually let him be home by five on weekdays and very seldom required him to work weekends. They had recently purchased a new home on a cul-de-sac. There were seventeen kids on their street, and most of them loved to hang out at Todd and Jessica's home. On top of all of those things, each of their children was involved in two outside activities, which usually meant two practices, one game, and one day for a music lesson—times three!

The first time I saw them in my office, I thought, *This couple looks really tired.* As we talked, I found out I was right. They told me they were tired and that they sometimes felt like strangers, which scared them. Todd said, "It doesn't seem that long ago that we were so connected; and then we had kids." I get that. Kids are one of the greatest blessings that God gives us in our marriages *but* they are also one of the greatest distractions from our marriages. Todd and Jessica did what almost every couple does as they enter the "raising children" stage of life: they forgot to prioritize their marriage. Connecting before kids had been easy, but now it seemed impossible. Welcome to life in the twenty-first century.

I asked them what they had recently tried. Todd said, "I try to ask her how her day went, but I know she thinks it is because I am supposed to, and usually she is right. I just want to check it off my list, and I almost never hear her response." Jessica said, "When we were close, I felt like I was completely involved in every part of Todd's life. When things went well for him at work, I knew and we celebrated every victory no matter how big or small. Now, since his office moved a year ago, I'm not sure I could find my way there."

As much as you may identify with Todd and Jessica, you may identify with this too: life was not always this way for them. I cannot tell you the number of couples for whom the words "we used to be so connected" are part of their first counseling visit. That's the bad news. The good news is that they know what to do. *You* know what to do. Connection is not an abstract idea. You used to connect, and many of you did it well. It just got squeezed out with the demands and busyness of life. That needs to stop. Look at it this way: Your marriage is the most important relationship you will have in this life next to your relationship with Jesus.

If your marriage fails, look at the fallout. It will be devastating to you, your spouse, your kids, and on and on. If, on the other hand, you say no to some activities for yourself, your spouse, and your kids, the fallout will probably be zero! When your kids roll into adulthood, what do you want them to remember? A terrible divorce, or parents who made their marriage a priority and thus provided a loving, secure home for them?

The next steps are yours.

- *First*, find an hour to spend alone together when you will not be interrupted. This is not a "date night" but a "work night," which will lead to more date nights!
- *Second*, commit to a daily time together. If you can't find more, start with five minutes. The big idea here is to commit.
- *Third*, brainstorm all the things you did through your dating years, engagement period, and the before-kids

time of your marriage that connected you when you were together. Write them down. What will fit into your daily time together? What would be great for future date nights? If physical touch is not on your list, add it. It can be sexual, nonsexual, or preferably both.

- *Fourth*, don't let anything get in the way. Make these new marriage-long habits.

For Nancy and me, connection time each day is a highlight. It was, and is, something we both look forward to. Our pattern before kids was to spend that time right after I got home from work. Someone told me a long time ago that the way a couple spends the first ten minutes in the evening together determines how the evening goes. I took that to heart. Did that mean that we never had arguments later in the evenings? Not necessarily, but I think there were fewer and they were less intense because of the way we spent our first ten minutes.

When our kids were little, it took more effort and often a little sacrifice. I made it a priority to find Nancy as soon as I got home. Sometimes I was walking with a kid on each leg or one in my arms and the other hanging on. I navigated around toys, dogs, etc., but I found her, kissed her, and asked how her day was. Our connection time during those years came after the kids were asleep. Someone wanted to know if we were tired during those years. The answer is yes, but we realized how important connection was for us. We looked at it this way: we could be rested and disconnected, or tired and connected. We chose tired, and looking back, that was a good choice.

## KEYS TO COMMONALITY

When our marriages get off track and stay there for a length of time, we get in trouble. Getting back on track and staying on track is never easy, but the end result is worth it.

As we complete this chapter, here are some things I want you to think about:

- Do you have common interests with your spouse? If yes, do you enjoy them together? If no, will you commit to working on developing these together over the next month?
- What needs to change in your lives to make room for more "common interest" time together?
- Have you started asking your spouse daily, "How can I help you?" If not, what is holding you back?
- Are the two of you committed to a daily connection time together? Have you started it yet? If not, how about starting today?

---

*Going Deeper*

Expand your daily time together to include a time for prayer. Don't let this be difficult. Start

---

simple. Decide on one thing you both want to pray for God to do in your marriage. Then pray and ask Him to do that. You can pray silently or out loud. You can both pray or one of you can pray. The really cool part is that you will see God show up. He wants to. When you go daily to Him in prayer together, watch out. Amazing things are going to happen, and you have taken a big step in avoiding a train-wreck marriage.

CHAPTER 2

# Wearing Their Shoes: Empathy

## LIFE REVERSAL

Even after counseling couples for thirty-plus years, I would never say that I can totally and completely understand how someone else is feeling. As a counselor, I listen well to people, accept where they are, and then help them toward healing. That works well for me at our counseling center. I don't have to put myself in their shoes to be a good counselor.

It's different for me at home. There are times when it is really beneficial to try to put myself in Nancy's place and imagine as best I can how she's feeling. Husbands and wives are different in so many ways. We have different perspectives. Our feelings and emotions and how we respond to the daily pressures of life may also differ. That's the way God wired us. We are different by design. The problems come when we begin to judge each other's differences. We may see the way we feel and respond to situations as the "right" way and see our spouse's way as wrong. That alone will usually cause conflict. There have been times in our marriage when I wished that God had made Nancy to feel and respond like I do. Just another good reason why I would make a terrible god. If we were the same, we would not experience the growth in marriage that these differences give us. I know that over the years of our marriage when we truly embrace our differences, we understand each other better, we grow individually, and our marriage grows.

It seems that most women are more relational than their husband. Some wives are a lot more relational! One of the areas of life where Nancy and I are different is in relationships. I do value my relationships with my friends, and most have been really good over the years. I have some lifelong friends I cherish. The same is true of Nancy and her friends. But we differ in how we handle conflict in those relationships.

If one of my friends says something harsh to me or does not show up when we are meeting for lunch, I am bothered but get over it pretty quickly. I will usually handle the situation by waiting a day or two and then contacting the person to talk things out. There is seldom much emotion on either side, and 90 percent of the time we work things out and are best buds again.

I remember in fifth grade having an argument with one of my really good friends. He wanted to meet after school to fight it out, and I was all in. The school day ended and I waited with some of my other friends on the playground.

He never showed. I was elated. A victory by default, and my other friends were there to witness the no-show fight. I got on my bike and, when I was about halfway home, there in the street was my no-show friend with the biggest and strongest guy in our class. The ensuing fight did not go my way because every time I was getting the best of my friend, the big guy stepped in. The fight finally ended with my friend sitting on top of me flanked by the big guy. Now what happened next I think is a great example of male and female differences with relationships. The big guy went home and left us. My friend and I lived close to each other. We began our journey home *together*. I walked my bike and he walked with me. By the time we reached our streets, we had our arms around each other. We stayed close friends for years.

The first time in our marriage that Nancy was emotional over a relationship with a friend, I handled it like a guy. I said things like, "Get over it," "She's not that good of a friend anyway," and "It's not worth getting upset about." I thought I solved her problem until she said, "You are not listening. I don't want you to figure this out for me. That's not what I need from you."

I give Nancy a lot of credit. She tried to tell me what she was thinking and feeling. I just did not hear her. I was so sure that she was making a big deal out of nothing that I basically ignored her. Honestly, in those early years of marriage, I was a slow learner. It took a long time before the idea came to me that her feelings and emotions and how she viewed situations might actually be valid. I think the difference came when I finally began to listen to her and tried to hear what she was saying.

Today there are still times that I do not get her responses, but I listen better. I consciously try to put myself in her shoes. I ask myself, "What does this situation look like through Nancy's eyes?" and "How is her perspective different from mine?" Those two questions, coupled with taking time to listen and process before I respond, have made a huge difference for us. I can truly empathize with her without judging.

What about you and your spouse? What if you took time to put yourself in their shoes? What if you really listened to them when they were sharing something with you that was important to them? What if you ask yourself how this looks through their eyes? What if you acknowledge that you would handle the situation in a different way but don't judge their way of handling it? It changed so much for me and my marriage. Why not try it?

## DAILY PRESSURES

Most of us would say we face pressure every day no matter what we do. In most marriages, both the husband and wife work. That seems to be especially true before a couple has children. After a child is born, if one is to stay at home, it is usually the wife. No matter which situation you find yourself in, there is daily pressure. There is pressure at work and pressure as a stay-at-home parent. In and of itself, this pressure is not necessarily bad, although it can be. When we had children, Nancy stayed home until they were in school and then she worked part-time. I think it took me a while to realize how much stress she experienced with taking care of first one and then two children. It was a job she loved, but there were lots of things to get done every day. Once she went to work, more pressure came as she was learning a career and at the same time giving it her very best at home.

It is obvious to most people that I love my work. In fact, I love it so much that I seldom think about it as work. Counseling with people and helping them see God's plan for their life and marriage is very rewarding. I love all I do with Awesome Marriage, as we tell people across the globe in many different ways about God's incredible plan for marriage. Yet there is pressure and stress. Every couple I counsel is different. Some are more challenging than others. I love writing but there are always deadlines. Every time we record a new podcast, I still get butterflies in my stomach, and the same is true when I speak at events. My point is that no matter how much we love our work, there will be pressures. If we don't really like our work, then the pressures are magnified.

Do you think that you have a good idea of the pressures your spouse faces each day? Do you understand the stress he or she is under? I think that far too often we keep these areas of our lives separate. We don't really engage with each other about what goes on each day at work in any depth. For the stay-at-home parent, it may be obvious that there is stress, but do we take the time to understand what they go through each day? Maybe we are even somewhat envious that they get to stay at home while we face the world every day.


## TOM AND ANN


Tom began working right out of college for a start-up company. The company was family owned, and Tom was their first outside hire. Over the next fifteen years the company experienced a consistent pattern of growth. With the growth came new opportunities for Tom. He knew the company inside out and was now in an executive position with an excellent salary. Tom and Ann dreamed for years of building their own home on a piece of land Ann's grandparents had left her in their will. Now seemed like the perfect time to take that step. Ann knew the architect and the builder she wanted them to use, and Tom was 100 percent on board. Their oldest child would be starting school shortly after they made the move. Everything was fitting together. It couldn't be better.

Tom and Ann had been living in their new home for about eight months when Tom began to hear rumblings around the office. The company's growth and sound financial base might have attracted a potential buyer. The rumor was the buyer was a big corporation that saw Tom's company as an asset to their growing portfolio. Tom had no idea what that might mean for him. Would this new company keep all of the employees? More importantly, would they keep him? What would his position

be? What about his salary? There were many more questions than Tom had answers for. That evening when Tom
went home, Ann asked him how his day was, and Tom
said, "Fine." He made the decision to keep all of his fears
to himself, never giving Ann the opportunity to share in
the pressures he was feeling.

It was two months before the impending sale of Tom's
company was public. About that time they came to see
me for counseling. As they sat down on the couch in my
office, Tom looked tired and weary. Ann was angry. Most
of Tom's fears were coming true, and he waited until near
the end before telling Ann. To some degree, Ann was
angry at Tom's company, but most of her anger was at
Tom for leaving her on the outside as things developed.
Ann sensed something was wrong at least a month before
the news was public, but when she asked Tom, he repeat-
edly said it was nothing. Tom was in a mess. His marriage
was in a mess and he still was not sure if he had a job.

I don't know what pressures Adam and Eve faced daily
in the Garden of Eden. I think just remembering the names
Adam gave to all the animals was a big task. What I do
know is that by spending time with them each day, God
showed us a model for relationships. We need to take time
to share the pressures and stresses of life with each other
and with God. It was impossible for Adam and Eve to hide
things from God, and the same is true for each of us today.
What if Tom had shared with Ann from that day when he
first heard the rumors? Would the two months have been
different? Ann thought so. Beneath her anger, she was sad

that she had not been able to walk through such a stressful time with Tom. She felt robbed of the opportunity she would have embraced to walk beside her husband through something challenging.

## RUNNING FROM GOD

When we have stress and pressure in our lives, we have a choice. Do we tell our spouse or not? We can make all kinds of assumptions, but we never know for sure what our spouse will do if we don't let them know what we are facing. It took me time to learn this. Maybe it was the male ego thing or fear of losing my "man card," but I thought I was supposed to handle things on my own. I would figure it out, I told myself. Yet I didn't.

I remember one time in particular that changed things for me. For the first twelve years of our marriage, I was running from God. Running from Him was not new for me. I felt called to ministry when I was twelve years old. It was so clear to me, and then life got in the way of my calling. Through high school and college, I bargained with God (not a good idea!). I graduated with a business degree, married Nancy, and continued my bargaining. For twelve years, I pushed back God's leading. I ran and ran and ran, yet God was everywhere. Nancy knew something was up, and finally I let it all out. I was scared. I did not want to tell her. I knew what going into ministry would mean for us. There would be big changes. Our income dropping about

75 percent while I went to seminary was at the top of my "how will she take it?" list. This was the sequence of the next three months of our lives:

- She suggested that I talk to a good friend of ours who was a Christian counselor to get his input and wisdom.
- I had lunch with that friend the next week. I laid out everything in front of him, and then he looked at me and said, "Have you ever thought about being a Christian counselor?"
- My answer was no, but an incredible peace came over me. This is what God was trying to get me to do. This is what I had been running from.
- My friend helped me decide on the education I would need and asked me to apply for an internship where he worked.
- Nancy and I went to dinner alone the next evening. I'll never forget that Tuesday night. We went to a little family-owned Mexican restaurant where we knew we could have some privacy. I told her everything I thought God wanted me to do: go to grad school, apply for the internship, and gradually back out of my work responsibilities. I told her we would have to live on a lot less money and that I thought many of our friends and family were going to think I had gone off the deep end.
- Then she looked at me lovingly with those blue eyes I fell in love with years before and said, "I am all in with you. Let's do this!"

- By that fall I was in grad school and beginning an intern-ship to learn about Christian counseling.

Would I have taken the step sooner if I had let Nancy in on what was going on earlier? I'm not sure because, looking back, the timing was perfect. Yet I do know the years lead-ing up to the decision would have been so much easier if I had included my soul mate in the journey.

How would you rate the two of you on your openness with each other about the stresses and pressures you face each day? How good are you at knowing when your spouse is feeling stress and pressure? What needs to change to bring oneness into this area of your marriage? What is a first step that you can take now?

## GIVING AND RECEIVING

Think about your marriage as you answer these questions. Is there balance in what you give and what you receive in your marriage? When you go through hard times, is your spouse there for you? Are you there for them when the situation is reversed? The ideal is that there is balance and that being there for each other during hard times is reciprocal. Let's unpack that.

When we got married, we were pretty selfish. Our unspoken motto seemed to be that if you do something for me, I might do something for you. There were strings attached to everything. We were twenty and twenty-two and trying to figure out life and marriage at the same time. We each had our list of expectations for each other that we never shared with each other. All of the above is what not to do, but all couples seem to fall into that pattern at least once in their marriage. We are selfish by nature. We want things our way. The idea of giving unconditionally is a novel idea for most of us, but an idea that Jesus touted throughout His earthly life.

I really don't know how much time I spent in those early years of our marriage waiting for Nancy to "get it," but it was a lot. I knew without a shadow of a doubt that when she was ready to do marriage my way, things would be so much better. If only I'd known that she was doing the same thing as she waited for me to get it! Looking back, I can see how patient God was with us. He gave us mentors who modeled marriage for us. We heard marriage sermons and went to a marriage event or two. Finally, I realized that I had to quit playing that game. There was no way I could justify it. Waiting for Nancy to "get it" was not a part of the covenant that I had made with her and with God. My job was to give. Period. I could not keep score. It did not matter whether she gave or did her part. That was between Nancy and God.

I wish I could tell you that I made this incredible turnaround and selfishness never reared its head again, but that would not be true. It was a process. It still is a process, but I am light-years away from where I was at age twenty-two. Now, here is the cool part. Once I began giving without strings attached, guess what happened? Nancy began giving without strings attached. For the first time in our marriage, I tasted what it meant to be a servant leader in marriage, and it was good. We were beginning to live out God's plan for our marriage. Sure, we take steps back, but we never have hit bottom again and we recover more quickly with every passing year.

Selfishness is not the only way that we can get out of balance. Sometimes things get out of balance for legitimate reasons. We had been married for seventeen years and Nancy was facing major surgery. We trusted the doctor and the hospital. Both had great reputations, but this surgery would keep her in the hospital for almost a week, and the recovery would be fairly painful and slow. I blocked out my schedule so that I could spend the week with her. My parents were in charge of the kids. The day of the surgery was a hot August day. Things went well and I spent the night at the hospital with Nancy. The next morning I went home to clean up and realized the air conditioner was out. The upstairs of our home was like an oven. Each day that week I reminded myself to call the air-conditioner repairman, and late each night as I sprawled on the bed when I got home, I knew I had forgotten again.

By the fourth day after surgery, Nancy was supposed to be getting better and she wasn't. In fact, that day she began to get worse. She could not eat and was drinking very little. She was losing weight and had no strength. She needed help to do everything. As the days passed, the doctors tried a number of things, but she kept getting worse. It was now day thirteen and I was watching her waste away.

Even though she was incredibly weak, the surgeon decided he had to open her up again. They scheduled the surgery for the first thing the following morning.

I was in a daze. I was sleeping in a ninety-degree bedroom at night. The rest of the twenty-four hours, I was living at the hospital. I was surviving on hospital-cafeteria and vending-machine food. I was barely seeing my kids and did not want them to see their mom like this. She talked to them on the phone, but talking wore her out. That morning after they took her into surgery, I went into the hospital chapel alone to pray. It seemed like forever when a nurse came to get me and said, "The doctors are wrapping up and want to talk to you in a few minutes." My heart sank as I followed her to the surgery waiting area. Finally, the two surgeons came walking toward me and they were smiling! Nancy was going to be okay. There was another issue that did not show up at first but now had been repaired. She would need rest and time but would fully recover.

That was when I learned that there would be times of imbalance in our marriage. There would be times when one of us was on the stretcher and the other was not. In those times we would give and give and give with no strings attached. It was fourteen years later when I went through a difficult period of depression. There were times when I could barely function. It was during those many weeks that Nancy was the giver. She was there in every way possible and expected nothing in return. It is interesting how those times of imbalance in our marriages actually lead to balance over the course of a marriage. When we are on the stretcher, we receive, and

when we are off, we have the opportunity to give. It's reciprocal and it is part of an awesome marriage.


### KEYS TO EMPATHY


As we complete this chapter, here are some things I want
you to think about:

- How are you doing with putting yourself in your
  spouse's shoes? Think about what your spouse is doing
  right now. What are they facing? How are they feeling?
  What is their perspective? What could you do to show
  them you care?
- Make a list of the things stressing or pressuring you
  today. Is there any reason that you could not share those
  with your spouse?
- How do you handle pressure? Do you bottle it up or
  let it out? If you let it out, whom do you tell? Is it your
  spouse? If you bottle it up, try to share one thing with
  your spouse as a starting point.
- How would you rate yourself as a giver? What would
  make you be a better giver?

---

*Going Deeper*

    Each of you take the list you made in the exercise
above and pick out one thing that is stressful or puts

---

pressure on you. Write that one thing down on a clean piece of paper and then exchange your papers. Read what your spouse wrote and then put yourself in their shoes. Write on the paper two things you think they may be feeling or thinking. Now write down something you can do as a giver for your spouse in this situation. After you both finish, exchange papers again so you both have your original paper. Read each other's comments and then share your thoughts.

# CHAPTER 3

# Marriage on Hold: Kids

## CHILDREN AT THE CENTER

In many ways, we create our own problems with our kids. It begins the day they enter this world. Literally everything revolves around them. Realistically, it has to: Babies do not begin life with any skills beyond eating, sleeping, crying, and messing up perfectly clean diapers. We are at their beck and call. It's easy to see how kids think the world revolves around them in those early years. Their known world is small; everyone and everything in it seems to be focused on them. Yet what is fine in the beginning needs to change over time. If it does not, couples run the risk of creating a home culture that is not healthy for anyone.

Robert and Carolyn were married four years when their first child, Matt, was born. They were ecstatic. Getting pregnant was not easy for them, and then Carolyn spent the last four months of the pregnancy in bed. Carolyn came from a big family. Her parents were great and she was determined to replicate what they did, or even take it up a notch or two. Robert came from a broken home and was raised by a single mom who was constantly stressed to provide and care for him and his little brother. Robert wanted to write a new script for himself as a father. For the first two years of Matt's life, everything seemed to go as planned. They parented well together and devoted themselves to making things perfect for Matt.

The second pregnancy was much easier for Carolyn, and baby Caroline joined the family when Matt was three. As most couples find, raising two children as opposed to one changes a lot of things. Before Caroline, life was pretty balanced for Robert and Carolyn. Sure, they were focused on Matt, but they still had time and took time for their marriage. Now things were different. The balance was gone and there were decisions to make that they did not even realize they were making.

Simply stated, a child-centered marriage occurs when a couple continues to let their lives revolve around the kids. In my experience, it is not a conscious decision. Usually a husband and wife want the best for their kids and do their best to make it happen, never realizing the toll it takes on their marriage. I think that if this happened all at once, it would get our attention. Instead small steps grow into bigger patterns. The kids' activities take first place and date nights hardly ever happen. The couple seldom talks about anything but their kids. They cannot remember the last time they got away "just the two of them." The constant focus on the kids has the parents completely exhausted much of the time. Finally, one of the parents wakes up, sounds the alarm, and hopes the other parent hears their cry for help. If they do, they can make some decisions together to bring balance back to the family and their marriage. If they do not, the couple and their marriage are headed for a potential disaster.

It took a while, but Robert finally sounded the alarm. Caroline was almost four and Matt was seven. Matt was quite the young athlete. It wasn't that he was so much better than the other kids on the teams; he just really loved playing sports. He wanted to be on a team for every sport, and many of them overlapped. The combination of practices and games, along with school and school activities, was daunting. Caroline was taking piano lessons and was in a beginners' gymnastics class. Her schedule was not yet overwhelming, but Robert could see where things were headed with future recitals and meets. He waved the red flag. At first, Carolyn did not see it. When she did, she chose to not listen to his concerns.

About a year later they came to my office. Robert was hoping for a miracle, and Carolyn was hoping I could talk some sense into him—two people in one marriage with two entirely different agendas for counseling. That is never a good recipe. Robert was not asking for everything to change. He wanted boundaries put in place with the kids' activities and some balance in their lives and marriage. I think that Carolyn saw his points, but she was very reluctant to make any changes. She firmly believed this was the season of their lives to put everything into the kids, and then when the kids left home, they could get back to their marriage. Robert felt that if they waited, there would be no marriage to get back to. Carolyn said that she just could not do that to their kids. It was a stand-off, so in essence Carolyn won. Nothing changed. A year later, they were divorced.

## A CROSSROADS

We were married five years when our son, Grant, was born. Julie came almost three years later. They truly became our world, but we knew that world had to include our marriage. I wish I could give you the formula for how we made it happen, but I cannot. It was never a checklist. I think it eventually became a lifestyle.

The one thing that got Nancy and me through many of the crises of marriage was being best friends. A few years ago in an interview, we were talking about one of the really tough times of our marriage when we were on the edge of divorce. Nancy was asked why she stayed. Her answer was awesome: "I didn't want to lose my best friend." That truth not only helped us weather the crisis, but it also caught our attention when life with kids got our marriage out of balance. We both found we had no time for our best friend.

Looking back, I think it helped us to watch parents who

had children before we did get caught up in the cycle of having their kids do everything so they would not "miss out" on anything. We were able to see couples in situations that we did not want to be a part of, but it was still not easy. Once our kids were old enough to do music, sports, and other activities, we had to constantly check ourselves. Every couple has to make the decision they feel is best for them. Some thought what we did was too much, while others could not believe that was all we were doing. We limited our kids to one sport and one other activity. To be honest, there were a few times that seasons overlapped, but only for a short time. It worked for us because we still carved out time for each other daily and for a date night weekly. We held that time together as sacred, and it made a huge difference in our marriage.

I hear some of you saying, "But we have three or four (or more) kids." I get that. What worked for us might not work for you. That is where you have to step up and be the parent! You have to be the ones who set the rules. You are the only ones who can see the big picture, and it is okay to say no. I promise you this: no matter how much your kids think they won't survive if they don't get to play this or be involved in that, they will.

We loved watching our kids perform, whether on a stage, field, or court. I coached soccer and softball and helped out with baseball. Nancy was involved with some other moms, organizing snacks and other things that helped a lot. Time spent with friends was also very impor-tant to us. As our kids got into activities, our friend group began to change since we were around many of the same parents at kids' activities. We found other couples who had similar values about balance and life. Some of those couples are still our best friends today. Activities gave us a way to spend time with them and each other while enjoying our kids.

Realizing that we had choices was huge for us. I talk to so many parents who do not see that perspective. If all their kids' friends are playing a sport, they think they have to say yes and let them play. But they don't. I counseled a couple last year who faced that dilemma. Their fifth-grade son made the decision to play fall baseball, which was great. A few weeks later he was asked to play on a flag football team with all of his friends. If they let him play, it went against everything they had committed to as far as balance. If they didn't let him play, they were the "meanest parents in history" (as defined by their fifth grader). They said no. I ran into the couple the following January and they were ecstatic. Saying no was the best parenting decision they'd made in a long time. Some other parents shared that their willingness to say no encouraged them to also say no. *And* they were no longer the "meanest parents in history"! As time passed, even their son saw the value in that "no."

You may be in the middle of that season of life with your kids, or you may not be there yet. Wherever you are, why not take the time to have that discussion? First, define the values you have for your marriage and your family. When it comes to kids and activities, what fits your values? What fits your marriage? Once you agree on that, the next step is a plan of action and accountability to make sure you stay in balance.

## THE PAUSE BUTTON

Our family of origin has a powerful effect on each of us. That was our textbook on what family is all about. We see our first models of parenting, marriage, and life within a family. Some of us had good or even great models; others did not. If you came from a home with good models, you are blessed. In today's culture I see many people who did not, but I have learned something really interesting. Even if your family of origin was a great model, that does not necessarily mean the model will work perfectly in your marriage. This can cause as many problems as coming out of a "bad model" family. That scenario was Nancy and me.

My family was almost perfect, and I knew if Nancy and I just laid the same template over our marriage, we would be well on our way to an awesome marriage. It did not work that way, beginning with the fact that Nancy was not my mom and I was not my dad. We had to find what worked for us, and that was going to be a different template. Over time, with a lot of work and conflict, we were able to bring some good things from each of our families into our marriage and then see what fit and what did not. What about your family of origin—especially when it came to parenting? What worked then? Will it work now? Most importantly, can you see the value of being on the same page as your parents?

## KRISTIN AND CHRIS

Kristin was waiting for the perfect man to marry. After college, she moved back home to live with her parents, who had an amazing marriage. In Kristin's mind, she was preparing herself for marriage by watching her parents and learning from them. The waiting was difficult at times, especially since many of her friends married right out of college. But once she met Chris, there was no doubt in her mind that this was the man God had for her.

Chris relocated and shortly afterward joined the church where Kristin and her family attended. They met at a singles' event and began dating the following week. Chris was a great guy and they really seemed to be a perfect match. Chris was from the Northeast and grew up very differently from Kristin. Not bad—just different. Chris was from a Christian family and held the same values Kristin held. The difference showed up in the way the two families did life from day to day. Chris's home had more rules and was very structured. He came from a home of all boys, while Kristin's was all girls. Kristin's home was very flexible and had few rules. The interesting thing was that each home worked for the family who lived there. Kristin and Chris each felt their family of origin was healthy and a great model. For the most part, they were right.

Chris and Kristin had three kids in five years, and the

family of origin differences began to show up. Kristin's parents put marriage first and kids next. Chris's parents had a philosophy that put the kids first and the marriage on hold until the kids left home. The way Chris and Kristin's kids were spaced, that would put the marriage on hold for twenty-three years! When I saw them for counseling, they were at odds and both were firm that their way was right. I asked them to set the kid issue aside for a time and see if we could get on the same page about what they both wanted in their marriage. Surprisingly, that was easier than I thought it would be. They both agreed on all the essentials. The difference was that Kristin thought they should be working on them now while Chris was fine with waiting. I guess that really wasn't just a difference; it was a marriage breaker.

They agreed to a compromise. Chris gave some and so did Kristin. I didn't. I was firm that they had to put time and effort into their marriage. It wasn't everything I wanted for them, but it was a place to start—and something they could agree on. I also asked them to pray for God's wisdom for their marriage and their parenting. As always, God showed up. It wasn't something miraculous, but over time Chris began to see the value of investing in his marriage. He reaped the results and, interestingly enough, began to see that his parents did have some real voids in their marriage. That was a big revelation for him.

Today Chris and Kristin still have some struggles, but they have much more balance than before. They don't have the same marriage as either of their parents. They are working on the marriage God designed for them and being the parents He is equipping them to be. Their marriage is healthier and so are their kids, who have the security of two parents with a marriage they have learned to cherish.

## STAYING STRONG

Recently we did a podcast for Awesome Marriage on the dangers of a child-centered marriage. My hope was that the podcast would be a wake-up call for some parents who were falling into the trap of putting the kids ahead of their marriage. We talked about God's plan for marriage and how that plan does not change when children are born. We talked about balance and how important that is for a family. We talked about how unhealthy it is for children to think the world revolves around them. Our discussion was focused on how to have a marriage that thrives, all while investing in kids and giving them all they need to grow into strong, God-loving adults.

I believe I'm in touch with culture. Through counseling, reading, and study, I have a real feel for the pulse of society. After the podcast aired, we were affirmed by many who listened, but criticized by others. It was like we had stepped on holy ground with our shoes on. We never back down on topics. We have covered many controversial topics, but we have never seen backlash like that. I was shocked. I did not realize I was stepping on a land mine by challenging the concept of a child-centered marriage. If you Google "child-centered marriage" like I have, you will find article after article warning about the dangers of this family style. It sends the wrong message to the kids and the wrong message about marriage.

Parents are the primary model of marriage for their kids. If we don't work at giving them a healthy model, they may never figure it out. I share this with you because you may be on the right path and putting balance in your marriage. You may be putting your marriage first. You may work hard at being great parents. You may do all of these and more, and someone—or many people—will say you are doing it all wrong. They may not walk up and confront you (or they may) but the not-so-subtle messages are everywhere. Here is a list of not-so-subtleties that have been said to parents I know:

- Did you know Bobby is the only boy not playing baseball this fall? If you don't start him in baseball now, he will be too far behind to ever catch up.
- All the girls in the class are playing soccer this spring.
- If you want her/him to really learn piano, you need to go to this teacher.
- If he doesn't play soccer year-round, he will fall behind.
- You mean your kids aren't doing any sports this summer?

These are only a few of the pressure points, but you get the idea. Often the pressure comes from our own kids, and they can be very convincing! Many kids want to do everything. I get that, but who really runs the family? Who makes the decisions? Who makes sure there is balance? It has to be the parents.

Amy and Brett came to talk to me about all of the above. They knew what they wanted for their family. They knew that after God, their marriage was to come first. They knew they wanted their kids to be involved in sports and activities, but with balance. They knew they wanted lots of family time. They didn't know how to remain true to the things they wanted. They needed to know when and where to draw the line and how to keep a thirty-thousand-foot perspective and not get lost in the day to day. I gave them just one piece of guidance and they took it from there. I said, "Why not start with the things you value the most? Put them on the schedule first; then fit the rest in if there is room." Then I added, "Rate everything on a one-to-ten scale with ten being the highest. Put your tens on first."

The next time we met, Amy and Brett brought one of those big oversized calendars. It was for the following month and was color coded. Blue was for the tens on their list. These went on the calendar first. Each other number had a color, and things were placed on the calendar in descending order. There were colors for ones, twos, threes, and fours, but none of them made it to the calendar. Here is what I really liked about their approach. It was visual for both them and the kids. In a family meeting, they let the kids help with the rankings. Brett said that after he explained to the kids what they were doing, they really got into the process. This is what amazed me: The only tens on the calendar were time for Amy and Brett, family time, and free time! Not one sport or activity garnered a ten.

Maybe you are thinking that this would never work for your family. They would never go for something like that. But what if? Will you ever really know until you try? Maybe you will have to exert a little more parental direction than Amy and Brett did, but that is okay. The last time I checked, you were still the parents. Look at it this way: If you don't take control, who will? Plus, if you, your spouse, and your kids are on the same page, it's a lot easier to stay strong when the pressure rises. What's keeping you from taking step one?

## KEYS TO AVOIDING A CHILD-CENTERED MARRIAGE

As we complete this chapter, here are some things I want you to think about.

- If someone on the outside took an honest look at your family, would they see it as child centered or as balanced, with the marriage as first priority?
- Where do you feel the most pressure to put your marriage on hold while raising kids?
- What do you see as the dangers of having a child-centered marriage?
- If you are totally honest with yourself, where are your

blind spots in keeping your marriage and family in balance?

- What is your next step in keeping the priorities for your marriage and family on track?

---

*Going Deeper*

If you never feel pressure to put the kids first, please write me and let me know where you live! In the culture where I live, that pressure always seems to be around for parents as they raise their kids. If you are to withstand the pressure, you need a plan. You need to be on the same page as husband and wife. Start with a thirty-thousand-foot list of the things that you want for your children from birth until age eighteen. Think about faith and values, and what you want them to learn and to experience. Those are your tens and need to remain tens year after year. Now you can add in the nines, eights, and sevens, and you have a road map to follow on the highway of raising a family. Your marriage will be better, and your kids will be healthier in every way.

CHAPTER 4

# Taking Care of You: Personal Health

## TWO SIDES OF HEALTH

Most people would agree that taking care of their health is important, yet most people struggle to do that with any consistency. We can find myriad excuses to justify our actions (or inaction). We know that smoking is terrible for our health, but people still smoke. Almost a half million people die from smoking every year. Then there is obesity. In October 2017, the Centers for Disease Control and Prevention reported that almost 71 percent of Americans are either overweight or obese, and the percentage is trending upward. Many experts are calling obesity an epidemic. It affects the way we feel about ourselves and the way others look at us and increases the risk for high blood pressure, diabetes, heart disease, and stroke. As a counselor, I know that there are many psychological reasons why people don't take care of themselves. I also know that there are solutions

to each and every one of these reasons. Far too few people make the choice to get help and turn their unhealthy
lifestyle around.

I smoked during, and after, college. I knew it was bad
for me but I was young and, in my mind, bulletproof. I
talked about quitting but didn't do it. I justified smoking because my friends smoked more than I did. I guess in some
strange way that made me feel better about my own habit.
All my excuses and procrastination went out the window
when our son was born. I put down the cigarettes and never
picked them back up. The decision was not for me but
for another human being. I was determined not to smoke
around my child and not to purposely do anything that
could shorten my life. Honestly, at that point it became an
easy decision. Maybe that is the way I am wired, because
I know that, for many, quitting is a difficult and lengthy
process. I definitely empathize; I also know that whatever it
takes to stop is worth it.

Let's look at the other side of the health issue. What are
the benefits of being healthy and taking care of yourself?
Most obviously, you will feel better. You will have more
energy and want to do more. You will look better. Sure,
we all age over time, but have you ever compared a healthy
person at any age to someone unhealthy at the same age? In
the vast majority of cases, there is a notable difference. You
will be doing your part to live longer. There are no guaran-
tees, but taking care of your health goes a long way toward
extending your life.

Those are some obvious examples that come to mind,

but there are many others. My point is that taking care of yourself has plenty of great benefits, while failing to take care of yourself has none. How would you rate your efforts at maintaining a healthy lifestyle? Are you doing all you can to stay healthy? What change could you make today that would be a step in the right direction?

## LOOKING GOOD

I once heard Pastor Tommy Nelson say, "We look the best ever on our wedding day and it is all downhill from there." While there is a certain amount of truth to that, we put way too much stock in what our culture calls attractive. Culture points at this fashion model, that movie star, or some athlete and says the goal is to look like them. Yet if we look behind the curtain, the image that's being presented is usually not the same as what is truly there. Photos are touched up, movie stars are made up, and athletes are pumped up. In other words, much of what we see is not real, but we keep buying into the idea that it is.

Our first step is removing the fantasy world from our idea of what is attractive. Look at it this way: Your spouse married you. Your spouse was attracted to you. You were—and are—enough. Though you may not look like you did on your wedding day, that does not mean you are on an inevitable downhill slide. We have to get past the images and lies that culture has filled your mind with. For your spouse and your marriage, you are more than enough. Your job is simply to take care of what you have.

This next part is for the ladies, but I want you men to read it too. It is so important for us as husbands to have an understanding of what our wives deal with when it comes to feeling attractive.

First and foremost, stop believing the lies. The "perfect woman" does not look like some model or movie star. The perfect woman is you! God created you perfectly and He made you perfectly for your spouse. God does not make mistakes. As long as you continue to believe the lie that you have to look like "that" to be attractive, you will stay on a never-ending quest of frustration and disappointment. On the other hand, if you embrace yourself as perfectly made by God, your inner and outer beauty will shine as never before. It's not an easy assignment. For some it will be a daily battle, at least for a while, but the results are more than worth all the effort.

I remember that for the hour before our wedding, I was sequestered in an oversized closet somewhere in the church where I was married. All my guy friends deserted me. My best man deserted me. They were all on "the outside" taking pictures and enjoying themselves. I was sequestered because no one wanted me to accidentally see Nancy before she walked down the aisle. That was really okay with me and I totally bought into it. What was not okay was that during that hour alone, all the fears of "what in the world am I doing?" flooded my mind. By the time my groomsmen and best man showed up, I looked fine on the outside but inside I was a mess. We lined up in a hallway waiting for our cue to walk into the sanctuary and take our places. We filed in as the organ began to play. I looked out at the sea of faces and watched the bridesmaids walk down the aisle, and then I saw the doors shut at the far end of the room. My heart was beating fast. I may have thought about running, but thank goodness the message never got to my feet. Then, in an instant, everything changed. The doors opened. Nancy and her dad began to walk down the aisle. My heart rate slowed and a peace came over me. I knew without a doubt "what in the world I was doing" there. Nancy did not just look beautiful; she *was* beautiful, and she was minutes from becoming my wife.

As Nancy approached forty, she went through a sort of "crisis" that seems to be an epidemic among women. She did not feel beautiful anymore. No matter what I said or how I said it, she just did not believe me when I told her she was beautiful. She was sure I was just trying to make her feel better, and there was no way I was going to convince her otherwise. Did she look like she had at twenty on our wedding day? No. Did she look like she had at thirty? No. Did she look a little different at forty? Yes, but what was so hard for her to accept was that I truly thought she was more beautiful at forty than she was on our wedding day. This is what I think so many women have difficulty with. While they look different at different stages of life, this does not mean they are not beautiful at each stage. It goes back to the cultural lies that we allow to define beauty for us. It took a lot of work on both our parts, but I think she finally came to a point where she could believe me and embrace the words I said.

The question we need to look at is this: Is keeping yourself attractive for your spouse a priority? Remember when you were dating? Remember thinking about what you were going to wear? As a guy, I showered, shaved, put on my favorite shirt, and washed my car. I wanted to look and smell my best for her. That first semester at college when Nancy and I were dating, I never saw her wear the same clothes twice. I thought the girls' dorms must have huge closets. What I found out much later was that at times she borrowed clothes from friends so I would always see her in something new. The point is that we both made a lot of effort then, and most of the time now we still make an effort. (Although I don't always wash my car!) We continue to make it a priority. We want to look our best for each other. Do we have to? No. But doing so adds something special to our marriage. I still get a spark every time Nancy walks into a room. I think she would say the same. I would never change that.

Nancy and I like to eat out. We like to try new places and explore new areas of town. We often find ourselves at restaurants with a lot of younger couples. Some are probably married; others are not. This is what drives me crazy. More often than not, we see several couples where the girl has obviously made an effort to look great for the date but the guy looks like he made no effort at all. I know this is partly due to culture, but I still don't have to like it, and I don't think it does anything to enhance or build a relationship. Guys, shape up!

## YOU ARE WHAT YOU EAT

My hands-down favorite vegetable is French fries. I could eat them every day and never, ever get tired of them. If I ate French fries every day, I know there would be consequences to the way I look and feel, so I don't. I have always wished that healthy foods tasted like unhealthy foods and vice versa. It would make those choices so much easier! We talked earlier about obesity and being overweight. There's not much more I will say about that, but it is a problem and it affects many people.

Garrett was a football player, and a good one. He received a college scholarship to play, and he loved the game. Not every college player gets to move on to the next level, and neither did Garrett. He left college in picture-perfect shape at six feet two inches and 220 pounds. He also left with a degree and had put an engagement ring on his girlfriend Amber's finger. Life looked very promising for the two of them.

Garrett continued to work out with some buddies for a couple of years, but life changed for many of them and the workouts finally came to a close. As an athlete, Garrett could eat about anything he wanted. Being very active combined with being young gave him a lot of flexibility in what he ate. Approaching thirty and working long hours without exercising did not give him that same flexibility, but eating habits are difficult to break. When I met Garrett, he was close to 300 pounds and not in very good shape at all. Amber was a combination of frustrated, angry, and sad. She married a guy who liked to look good for her and liked to do things with her.

Now Garrett didn't care much how he looked, and he'd rather sit on the couch watching sports than get up to do things. Their lifestyle had changed. For Amber, it was never a deal breaker, but she wanted so much more. I worked with them to restore their connection, which had dwindled to almost none. I referred Garrett to a dietician, a doctor specializing in obesity, and a physical trainer. We had a good game plan but the ball was in Garrett's hands.

The next year was tough. Garrett changed the way he ate, dealt with some resulting health issues, and began the task of getting back into shape. Amber was all in. She became his cheerleader, and together they made amazing progress both in their marriage and in Garrett's health. After twelve months, Garrett's weight was under 200 pounds, his eating was much more balanced, and the gym had a permanent spot on his calendar. I asked Garrett what he had learned and what he would share with others. Here is his list:

- If you are in shape, keep at it.
- Balanced eating needs to be a lifestyle. The dietician

taught him that he did not have to avoid all the things he loved to eat. He just needed to balance the foods.

- If there is a health issue, the sooner you face it, the better. Don't procrastinate.
- Never take your spouse for granted. Continue to pursue them every day.

Not a bad list. What can you learn from Garrett's story? What change would make a difference for you and for your marriage?

## THE GYM

By the end of our first year of marriage, Nancy and I were in the worst physical shape we had ever been in and weighed more than either of us had ever weighed. We never watched what we ate. Nancy cooked some amazing things but most were not the healthiest. The only exercise we got was sex, and that was not shedding any pounds for us. We finally figured out that something had to change. I think the big wake-up call came when we both had more clothes that didn't fit than ones that did. We were on a limited budget, and weight loss was a better and cheaper idea than buying new clothes. The big thing for us was that we were totally on the same page and were committed to beat our weight gain together. Nancy cooked healthier foods, and I learned to love what she made. We joined a gym, which was huge for us. I had not worked out consistently since playing high school sports, and Nancy had never really had an exercise plan. Our schedules did not allow us to work out together. I found that working out early in the morning worked best for me. Nancy liked working out a little later in the morning. Even though we went at different times, there was the built-in accountability of each asking, "Did you work out today?" Working out became a lifestyle for us. Nancy enjoyed classes like aerobics and also used weights. I became a runner and worked with weights. After running in high school, it was hard for me not to get competitive, so I would compete in a few races every year. There have been so many benefits for us in consistently exercising. The obvious one is that we look and feel better. We have more energy and we are healthier. When we get sick or have surgery, we always recover ahead of schedule. The benefits are endless.

What do you need to do? Beginning an exercise program is easy. Being consistent with exercise over a lot of years is difficult, but don't start there. Start with a three-month plan and then evaluate it. Decide what you are going to do. I think part of the reason I picked running for so many years was that it was easy for me. I just rolled out of bed, threw on some running clothes and shoes, and hit the street in front of my house. I was usually back before anyone else was up at home. As I continued running, I began to have some nagging injuries, and I talked to an orthopedic doctor who was also a runner. I learned early on to not go to an orthopedic that was not a runner because he will tell you to stop running. My doctor encouraged me to begin a weight program to strengthen muscles and help prevent injury. I did, and it worked.

Running is not for everyone, so I am not pushing it. Nancy and a lot of women that I know love classes. Nancy likes to exercise but she also likes the social aspect. Classes give her both. The idea is to find something you think you will like and stick with it. After three months you can decide to keep doing the same thing or alter your program. An interesting thing happened to me. I am really not sure when it occurred, but I realized one day that my body was craving exercise. Maybe it was the runner's high, but whatever it was helped immensely with motivation.

I know a number of really good personal trainers. They design your program and constantly evaluate you and your progress. There is also built-in accountability, which always helps. A trainer may be a great way for you to start and get in the exercise routine. Bottom line: just start. If you are overweight and out of shape, start slowly, but start. It is always a great idea to see a physician before you start an exercise program.

Has exercise made our marriage better? Yes. Has it made us bulletproof? No. We still get sick. I'm a cancer survivor, and at one time Nancy had a heart issue. Exercise is not a miracle formula, but being healthier and feeling good has been a real blessing in our marriage.

It's your turn. What do you need to do? It's easy to

procrastinate when it comes to exercise, but procrastination will not get the job done. It's time to take that first step—literally!

SLEEP

For most of my life, I have slept well. I go to sleep quickly and if I wake up in the middle of the night, I usually go right back to sleep. I wake up easily and hit the ground running. I know. Many of you hate me right now. You are in good company because Nancy is on your team. Sleep is often elusive for her. It used to make her mad that I could lie down and be asleep in less than ten minutes. It only became a problem for me when she would want to talk in bed and I would fall asleep in the middle of her sentence, but that is for another chapter.

It is not rocket science to know that sleep is important for us. Sleep gives the body time to recover from the previous day. How well I perform tomorrow depends a lot on how well I sleep tonight. The National Heart, Lung, and Blood Institute lists many benefits of sleep:

- Sleep helps your brain work properly.
- Sleep improves learning.
- Sleep helps you pay attention, make decisions, and be creative. Lack of sleep does just the opposite.
- Sleep is involved in the healing and repair of your heart and blood vessels. Sleep deficiency is linked to an in-

creased risk of heart disease, kidney disease, high blood pressure, diabetes, and stroke.

- Sleep helps you function throughout the day.
- The recommended amount of sleep for adults eighteen years and older is seven to eight hours a night.

What if we take that list of benefits and apply them to your marriage? If you get enough sleep, you will both think more clearly, do a better job of listening to each other, and make better decisions as a couple, and your bodies will be healthier, giving you a better quality of life together. Most of the time you will come home in the evening with energy to spare.

How are you doing with this sleep thing? My experience is that most of us don't get enough sleep; therefore, we don't function as well as we could during the day, which can be frustrating. By the time we are together again as a couple, our tank is pretty empty. We can handle that for a short time, but if it goes on very long, it will begin to take a toll on the marriage.

When I can get couples to be honest with me about why they are not getting enough sleep, most of the time these are the answers I get:

- Surfing the internet
- Channel surfing
- Looking at social media
- Looking at YouTube videos
- Watching Netflix

None of those are essential! Believe it or not, you can live without any of them. Here is my challenge to you. For thirty days try this: First, decide what time you need to get up in the morning. Now back off eight hours, and that is your bedtime. By using eight hours as your standard, you have some margin that you would not have with seven. Finally, and this is really important, go to bed together. (Make this happen unless you work opposite shifts.) There are so many benefits to going to bed at the same time besides sleep. We will talk about some of those in a later chapter. At the end of thirty days, talk it over. Are you getting more sleep? Is your quality of life better? Is your marriage better? Hopefully you just answered yes to all three questions.

## JACK AND KENNEDY

When I think of personal health and how it affects a marriage, Jack and Kennedy always come to mind. They were in their early forties when I met them. They had been married for almost twenty years and had three children. Their oldest was a high school senior. The middle child was in eighth grade and the youngest was in fifth grade. In many ways they were a typical middle-class family. Jack had worked for the same company for twenty-three years. He had a great job that paid well but was high stress. Kennedy worked from home with a part-time job that allowed her to do the things she wanted to do as a mom.

The kids were active, but they seemed to have a good handle on balancing their activities. It helped that the oldest drove and could assist with transporting the other two. All in all, things had been good throughout their marriage. When they came to see me for counseling, there was no big issue. No fights, no infidelity, no drug or alcohol problem. But if things did not change for Jack and Kennedy, they were headed for a "dead marriage," a marriage that functioned like everything was okay but had no life inside. Their marriage was in a slow downward spiral, and they had no idea how to stop the slide.

I asked them a series of questions:

How much sleep do you usually get?

- Both said four to five hours but that they tried to catch up on the weekends.

How well do you eat?

- They looked at each other and actually laughed. It had been a topic of conversation before. Way too many meals were fast food as they rushed from one thing to another.

Do you weigh more than you did ten years ago?

- I always hate to ask a woman that question, but Kennedy did not hesitate in saying, "Absolutely." Jack too.

Do you exercise?

- Both said they used to, but it had been a long time.

Do you fight?

- No.

Do you communicate?

- Yes, but we are usually too tired.

The great thing about Jack and Kennedy was that they knew there was a problem and they wanted their marriage and life to be better. They were just so physically down they could not see the problem in front of them. We set a plan for change and once we got going, they had great ideas. They were determined to get healthy, and they did. I wish I had taken a picture of them the first day I saw them, because a year later they did not look like the same couple! They are a perfect example of how personal health problems can affect a marriage. Jack and Kennedy fought and won. What about you?

### KEYS TO PERSONAL HEALTH

As we complete this chapter, here are some things I want you to consider.

- How would you answer each of these? Yes or no:
  - I consistently get seven to eight hours of sleep.
  - I try to eat healthfully most of the time. When I splurge, I balance it out.
  - I exercise at least thirty minutes, three times a week.
  - I try to look my best for my spouse every day.
- As you look at your answers, prioritize what you would like to work on.
- Together make a game plan.
- How will you support each other as you implement your plan?
- How will you be accountable?
- How will you celebrate your success?

---

*Going Deeper*

In my opinion, this is such an important chapter. It can make a real difference in your life and marriage. It is one of the things that Nancy and I did right. We know how important it is. I know many couples quite a bit younger than Nancy and me that ignored all the warning signs and didn't make health a priority. You can get by with it for a while, but over time it catches up with you. So this is to encourage you to finish what you started and then to make it a lifestyle. Set a time each year to evaluate yourselves on personal health issues. Hold each other accountable. And most of all, enjoy the fruits of your hard work!

# CHAPTER 5

# Things That Take Away: Addictions

## WHAT-IFS

As a counselor, I don't deal directly with addictions. That is not my area of expertise, and I learned years ago to leave them to those trained specifically to deal with them. What I do see in the counseling room is the fallout of an addiction for a spouse and a family. It is devastating and honestly difficult to understand. Spouses have asked me, "Why is my spouse's addiction more important to them than I am?" It is a question I cannot answer, but that is their reality. I have never talked to someone with an addiction who set out to become addicted. It was never their intent, but that's what happened.

Paul had never been to a casino in his life until one opened in his town. It was huge, with the bright lights and all the associated fanfare. Paul decided he would check it out. What would it hurt to go one time? I get that. I'm not saying that walking in the doors of a casino is wrong at all, but it is important to know that there are some risks. I first talked to Paul about three years after that first time. He was now divorced and his daughters did not speak to him. He lost his good job and then a number of not-so-good jobs. He lost their dream house and their cars. When his wife finally filed for divorce, the process was simple. There was nothing left to divvy up.

The day I saw Paul, he had just finished two weeks in a new job. He was going to get his life back. He got his first paycheck the night before our appointment. He was going to use part of it to pay for counseling. When he left work that evening, he should have turned right to go home to his apartment, but instead he turned left to the casino. He lost every penny of that paycheck. The following day Paul told me his story. One thing really stood out. He said, "I think I would have been fine that first time going to the casino, but I won. I won big, and I felt something trigger inside of me. I could not stay away after that, even as I was losing everything that was important to me." I referred Paul to a counselor who specializes in gambling addiction, and he joined a Gamblers Anonymous group. We continued to meet to help him work on his relationship with his daughters. It was going to be a long, hard road for Paul.

Allison knew her dad had a drinking problem as she was growing up, but he always seemed to control it. She knew that at times he hid his drinking from her mom, though other times he would drink openly. He had a good job and was very successful. They had a nice home, and he was a really good dad and provider. She knew her parents' marriage wasn't great, but she knew her mom adored her dad. Allison never really understood the term "functional alcoholic" until many years later when she realized she was one.

Allison and Dan met in college and dated three years before they married. They both drank but so did everyone in college. Allison sensed her drinking might be a little different than Dan's. She seemed to look forward to it more than he did, and she often drank more than Dan. He never said anything about it, and neither did she. After they married, they both worked and really only drank on the weekend, and it was usually a glass or two of wine with dinner. Allison got off work an hour before Dan and started meeting a girlfriend for a glass of wine. She still got home at about the same time as Dan. He knew she did it a time or two each week but had no idea it had evolved into an everyday thing. Allison was still this perfect wife, was great at her job, and maintained her friendships. She could handle the drinking. Anytime she began to think she had a problem, she could find a reason why she did not. When she was pregnant with their first child, she stopped drinking for over nine months. She did the same with their second and third children. She was now a stay-at-home mom. She missed her friends and began asking them to drop by after work for a glass of wine. That went on for months.

One evening as Dan was tucking their oldest, Anna, into bed, Anna said something that got his attention. "Daddy, sometimes Mommy acts funny in the afternoon after her friends leave." Dan decided to not say anything to Allison since he was leaving the next day on a three-day business trip. He would sit down with her when he returned. The business trip went well and Dan was able to come home a day early. He decided to surprise the family. Dan walked in the house to find the kids in a panic and Allison passed out drunk on the bed. Dan called me and I connected them with someone to assess Allison and recommend treatment. Allison was broken and compliant and left for a three-month stint at a rehab center. I connected Dan with a counselor to help him understand Allison and to get him into a support group. Dan and I then met to talk about his marriage. He felt like it was just one big lie and said he had no idea who Allison was. Even if she got better, he was not sure he could ever trust her again as a wife and mother.

The number of people addicted to prescription drugs is astounding. Many start innocently. They have surgery and take pain pills for a few days; then the few days turn into weeks, then months. They seem to like the feeling they get from the pain pills or the ability the pills give them to not feel. Either can become addictive.

Sam was a well-respected general surgeon. He was always cautious when prescribing pain pills and warned his patients of the potential dangers. It was just after Thanksgiving and Sam was putting Christmas lights up on the house. As he climbed up the ladder, he thought to himself, *What in the world am I doing on this ladder?* A few minutes later the ladder tipped sideways and Sam fell, landing flat on his back. A trip to the ER confirmed that nothing was broken, but he was in a lot of pain. Sam took a few days off, and his office rescheduled surgeries. Sam stayed in bed flat on his back and took pain pills as often as possible. The following Monday, Sam was in the office seeing patients all day and had no surgeries scheduled. He knew he shouldn't but did not know how he could make it through the day without pain pills. You can probably guess what happened next. Sam continued to work, seeing patients and performing surgeries while on pain pills. He knew he was addicted but felt trapped. He just couldn't tell anyone. He would lose his medical license.

Sam didn't tell anyone, but people started observing his behavior, and he was finally confronted. Sam lost his medical license. His clinic paid for him to go to treatment, but the process to get his license reinstated would be long and difficult. There was really no guarantee that he would ever get it back. Sam's wife and family stood by him, but life changed drastically for them. I met Sam and his wife after he returned from treatment, as we began to work on their marriage and rebuilding trust. They had to sell their home and trade down on cars, and Sam was working retail to make ends meet. Sam told me he had never taken a pain pill before his fall, but he knew after a few weeks it was going to be very difficult to stop. If only he had asked for help then.

Prescription drugs, alcohol, and cocaine are just a few of substances that can be addictive. Addictions kill people and relationships. If there is, or ever has been, addiction in either spouse's family, you both need to know. The risk is higher with an addiction history. The addictions were different for Paul, Allison, and Sam. Their one similarity was that they all hid it. Look back at each story. What if Paul had talked to someone who understood gambling addiction after that first night in the casino? What if Allison had shared her feelings with Dan about her drinking early in their relationship? What if Sam admitted the pills were a problem before ever going back to work? The main thing I want you to get from these stories is that you don't have to be a what-if. If there is an addiction issue with you, your spouse, or both of you, begin reaching out for help now.

## LOVE THAT ADRENALINE

Adrenaline-producing behaviors can be every bit as addictive and damaging as substances. They just play out differently. We already talked about one through Paul's story. Paul's quest for the rush that came with winning began to trump everything else in his life. Other adrenaline-producing behaviors include porn, shopping, extreme sports, risk taking, social media, and video games. I know I just stepped on some toes, so let's unpack this.

First and foremost, we are talking about "things that take away," things that prevent a marriage from being everything God designed it to be. Granted, there are other things that can take away from a marriage. The difference here is that these can be addictive. Why? The person sees them as rewarding and reinforcing—a combination that allows for the very real possibility of developing an addiction to that behavior. Ruth C. Engs, in her article "What Are Addictive Behaviors?" discusses the theory that these behaviors may produce beta-endorphins in the brain, which makes the person feel "high." If a person continues the behavior, they may get into an addictive cycle. The person becomes physically addicted to their own brain chemicals, thus the behavior continues despite any negative health or social consequences.

Shopping is a part of our culture. It is an acceptable behavior, but what happens when someone gets this addictive high from shopping? What happens when this person runs up credit card debt and spends money they don't have? What happens when their spouse finds out? The cultural norm of shopping can put a dent or even a really big crater in a marriage.

In counseling, I see people engaging in potentially addictive behaviors all the time. Does everyone who looks at porn, uses social media, or plays video games become addicted? No. What about extreme sports and risk-taking behaviors? No. But is there a possibility of developing an addiction to any one of these? Yes. Absolutely, yes. Does each one affect a marriage in the same negative way? No. Some are more harmful than others. Let's look at three of these and the ways I have seen them negatively affect marriages.

### Video Games

The Illinois Institute for Addiction Recovery website gives us this definition of video game addiction:

Video game addiction is described as an impulse control disorder, which does not involve use of an intoxicating drug and is very similar to pathological gambling....

Similar to other addictions, individuals suffering from video game addiction use the virtual fantasy world to connect with real people through the Internet, as a substitution for real-life human connection, which they are unable to achieve normally....

Statistics show that men and boys are more likely to become addicted to video games versus women and girls. Recent research has found that nearly 1 in 10 youth gamers (ages 8–18) can be classified as pathological gamers or addicted to video gaming.

Video games are big business and they are not going away anytime soon, if ever. Since the statistics tell us that most guys start playing video games at a young age, the addiction is something they usually *bring* into a marriage rather than *acquire* in marriage. Probably not true 100 percent of the time, but it has been the case in my experience. While it may not have been an issue for someone living the single life, it can certainly be an issue in marriage. Often in a healthy marriage, both husband and wife have hobbies that their spouse is not interested in, so they work out time for each other to enjoy their activities. It becomes unhealthy only when those activities constantly take time away from the marriage. It's when things get out of balance that the problems begin. Ella and James are a great example.

Before marriage, Ella knew that James enjoyed video games. He and his virtual buddies spent lots of time playing. When a new version of their favorite game came out, they would spend a solid weekend playing. James always minimized it and worked at giving Ella time, but she could not help wondering if James was willing to curtail this behavior in marriage as he had said he would. Things went well the first few months of marriage. But then James's time playing games began to increase. It was shortly after their first anniversary that they came to me for counseling; James was spending most of his evenings with a controller in his hand. He had all the classic warning signs of addictive behavior:

- He thought about the game almost all the time.
- To get his "fix," he had to increase his playing time again and again.
- Even though he knew it was a problem for Ella and would say he was going to cut back, he didn't—couldn't.
- It was hurting their marriage. From Ella's perspective, it seemed he did not care.
- He lied to Ella, their friends, their parents, and to me about how much time he was really playing.

I saw a couple of things in James that were of concern. First, he did not see it as a problem. As we all know, the first step to addressing an addiction is admitting that you have a problem. Some of James's thinking was that because video gaming had been a part of his life for so long, he easily cast it as Ella's problem, and therefore came to counseling to help her. Second, he was able to justify his dishonesty within himself. He really thought that if Ella believed his lies about how much he was playing, everything would be okay. I knew that until James was ready to deal with these two issues, nothing was going to change. Ella asked him to move out until he was ready to be honest and deal with his addictive behavior. She said it was the hardest thing she had ever done, but she knew it was her only choice. What would you do if you were in Ella's place?

### Porn

Porn is a part of our culture. It is easily accessible, and our society as a whole does not frown on it in the way it did in previous generations. The media does its best to tell us that looking at porn is normal. It is talked about in sitcoms, often as casually as what's for dinner. Everybody does it! In the counseling room, I see a very different perspective. Let's look at Elizabeth's story.

Elizabeth's first pregnancy was a breeze. Almost every day she felt great. She and her husband, Jacob, seemed to grow even closer and their sex life hardly missed a beat. Then came the second pregnancy. It was tough, and neither she nor Jacob was prepared for what she went through. Even though Jacob said he understood, Elizabeth sensed something was wrong. He was different. He seemed distant. Elizabeth had nine months of morning sickness and was exhausted. Sex was not on her mind, but it was on Jacob's—at least in the beginning. Elizabeth tried to put in the effort, but was too sick, tired, or uncomfortable. Jacob quit trying. Now the baby was almost six months old and Elizabeth was more than willing, but Jacob didn't seem to be that interested. It was not that they never had sex, but it was infrequent and Jacob always seemed to hurry it along.

One night Elizabeth woke up at about three in the morning and reached over to touch Jacob, but he wasn't there. She figured he'd gone to the bathroom, but after about fifteen minutes, she got up to look for him. What she found shocked her. Jacob was downstairs in his study, naked, looking at porn. He was so into what was on the computer screen that he did not realize Elizabeth was in the room until she shrieked and ran out. Elizabeth tried to make sense of something she couldn't get her mind around. Yes, their sex life had suffered during the pregnancy and had not gotten back to where it had been, but he knew she was willing. She thought over and over, *Why would he go to that when he has me?*

That next morning Elizabeth called my office, and I agreed to meet with them later that week. As we talked in our counseling session, Jacob told me his story. The porn began during the pregnancy. He said he justified it easily since he and Elizabeth could not have sex, and then the pattern began. It was easily accessible and he had plenty of opportunities. What he didn't count on was the "high" that came with the behavior. There was a thrill he had not experienced before. He knew it was wrong and that it would hurt Elizabeth if she found out, but he could not stop himself. Now he had a decision to make: get help or get out.

Honestly, if a guy told me he had never looked at porn in his life, I would have a hard time believing him. My experience tells me that many men have looked at porn and then walked away from it. They didn't get the "high." They realized porn was a really cheap substitute for sex within marriage where there is freedom, commitment, and no guilt. Jacob pursued the behavior, and the addiction grew. It was about a year after that first counseling appointment with Elizabeth and Jacob that he told me getting caught was the best and worst thing that had ever happened to him. The best part was that he got help and was finally freed from the behavior. The worst part was the pain he saw in Elizabeth. Her healing had been, and still was, a long process. Things were better and they were on the right path, but rebuilding trust was a difficult process.

Let's talk straight here. In the past I would have aimed this mainly at the guys. But new studies say that now up to 30 percent of porn addicts are women. This is for all of us.

- Porn drastically distorts the sexual relationship designed by God. Don't buy into the lie that sex God's way is not fulfilling. The exact opposite is true. God's design is the most fulfilling sex imaginable.
- It is a temporary fix for a much bigger issue. Temporary fixes never solve problems. They actually help you ignore the real problem and keep you from dealing with it.
- Porn images hang on for a very, very long time.

- Porn keeps you from having a normal, healthy sexual relationship.
- Like any addiction, porn breeds dishonesty.

As a Christian, I do not think there is any way to justify porn being a part of your life. God tells us "to flee sexual immorality." His Word could not be any clearer. Whether you are a man or a woman, if porn is an issue for you, today is the day it stops. Today is the day you confess to your spouse and begin the process of healing. You will need help. First God, then others. Get the best help available. You are playing with fire here, so treat it as such. You will never regret taking that step.

### Social Media

An article by Bradford Health Services titled "Social Media Addiction: Genuine Disorder or Joke?" specifies this criteria: "The primary hallmarks of addiction are that a behavior is negatively impacting your life and you are unable to modify the behavior." They go on to say, "One thing is clear; if your or a loved one's habits are interfering with daily life and change is impossible, even in the face of negative consequences, then there is a problem. It is time to seek professional help and reclaim a happy, healthy life once more." The key for me here is the phrase "change is impossible."

Today many people let social media interfere with life in general, but it is a choice and they know it is a choice. In my opinion, that is not addictive behavior, but it can still have consequences for a marriage and family. The couple who gets in bed at night only to spend the time on social media that used to be spent in conversation will see a disconnect over time. Don't get me wrong, there are a lot of great things about social media. We can keep up with friends and their lives. We can find old friends. We can share with people we never would have shared with in the past. At Awesome Marriage, social media is one of the main ways we share and communicate God's incredible plan for marriage. *Balance* is the key here. It is knowing when to be on and when to get off. It's making the right choice each and every time. If the right choice isn't made, the door is wide open to problems—and for some the very real possibility of addictive behavior.

Nancy and I both spend time on social media but for different reasons. Nancy enjoys the social aspect and keeping up with people. She does a lot more "liking" than sharing but really enjoys looking. Most of my social media centers on Awesome Marriage. I spend very little time on it for myself. No matter the reason, we began to realize that when we were "on," we were basically "off" everything else. In fact, there were many times one of us was "on" and the other was talking. It was like talking to a wall. Neither of us heard a word the other said. That was not good. What started as a minor issue was growing into a much bigger issue. What finally got our attention was becoming aware of the fact that each of us got irritated when the other interrupted. We were putting social media over each other. We knew that we needed to make some changes. They were pretty simple but made a huge difference: We agreed to not be on social media for the most part when we were together. That included when we were at home, out driving, on dates, and any other time that we had an opportunity to connect. We also gave each other permission to call the other one out when we slipped back into the old behaviors—which we did. Overall, it has made a difference. Becoming aware of the problem and then taking quick action was a pivotal step forward for us.

Social media is a relatively new phenomenon for all of us. Many of us did not deal with it for a large part of our lives. It has been such a culture changer, and developed so quickly, that most of us were swept up in it without realizing what was happening. We all need time to slow down and take charge. What does balance look like? Are we in balance or out of balance? If we are out of balance, how far out? Where are you with the whole social media conversation? How is it affecting your life? What about your marriage? What do you need to do? You may be using it to fill a void in your life that you expected your spouse to fill. If that is the case, more social media is not the right answer. Instead, talk to your spouse. Express what you want and feel you need. Then seek help. If you try to stop and find you cannot, get help. Don't let the problem persist. It will not get better on its own.

KEYS TO AVOIDING ADDICTION

As we complete this chapter, here are some things I want you to think about:

- We covered a lot of issues in this chapter, from drugs and alcohol to porn and video games. I think it is easy to begin to access these addictions in our minds and rank some as more important than others. Granted, the consequences of the varied addictions are different, but when we talk about how they affect marriage, I have seen couples divorce for every one of these addictions. Anything that takes you away from your marriage is a problem.
- If there is a history of addiction in your family, how are you dealing with that reality?
- Does your spouse exhibit behavior changes that could be related to substance abuse? If so, what do you need to do?
- Is your spouse possibly addicted to adrenaline-producing behaviors? Is so, what do you need to do?
- If your spouse is in denial, what do you need to do for yourself?
- Take an honest inventory of your social media life and see if you need to begin making changes.

---

*Going Deeper*

    As an author and a counselor, I can take you only so far here. I can address the problems and tell you about the consequences I see. I can talk to you about warning signs and encourage you to take action. I can help you stay focused on the important things and people that God has put in your life, knowing that if you keep the focus, many of these issues will not become a problem for you. I can't help you with treatment, but there are many fine counselors, doctors, facilities, and treatment centers that can and will. Going deeper here is twofold. First, everything we talked about in this chapter can hurt your marriage even if it is not an addiction. Again, it goes back to keeping balance in your life and your marriage and staying away from things that could destroy either. Second, if this has raised a red flag for you and there is evidence of addiction, please take that first step by admitting there is a problem and asking for help.

# CHAPTER 6

# Friends or Foes:
# Conflict Behavior

Being on the same team" and "fighting for your marriage" are terms I use frequently because I know how hard
it is to do either consistently. Being on the same team is
an easy sell when I talk to couples. It is what they have
always wanted for their marriage. The concept of fighting together for your marriage instead of weakening your
marriage by fighting against each other just makes sense.
Often, though, things break down as a couple seeks to
live these ideas out day after day. It's a constant battle not
to fall back into old patterns. Nancy and I fight the same
battle. Of all people, we should and do know better, but
if we are not diligent, the human condition of selfishness
comes between us, and we find ourselves in separate cor-
ners ready to fight each other instead of fighting together.
In this chapter, I want to show you some consistent issues
that can come between a husband and a wife.

UNDER THE RUG

Picture this scenario: There is an issue in your marriage that you know is significant to you and your spouse. You know the best course of action is to set aside time to discuss it with your spouse, but things have been going so well lately that you just do not want to rock the boat. Then the season of "going well" ends and you are fighting over the very issue you put off discussing. Now it's a hot topic. Instead of talking about it rationally, the gloves are off. If only you had followed through before! Does this sound familiar?

Nancy and I were masters of this for years. We repeated the cycle over and over. We made pacts with each other to address issues when they came up and pursue them until resolved. That hardly ever worked because we would wait until we were both heated over the issue before attacking it. It was frustrating for both of us. At times we both thought we would never figure out how to handle conflict well. If we had continued the same pattern, we would have been right! Avoiding the important topics and sensitive issues in your marriage may not kill it, but it will limit how great your marriage can be.

There were a number of reasons Nancy and I struggled with this. First, we are both type A and stubborn. This meant that admitting we were wrong or listening to someone else's perspective did not come easily. Both of us thought things would be so much easier if the other would just do things our way. Problem solved! That was never, ever going to happen. Second, we were really busy with life, kids, and other things, and it was easy to take the focus off what we needed to do and just focus on what we wanted to do. We would go along pretty well for a while, and then one of our unresolved issues would come up again and we were back to square one.

Actually, we found we were a little behind square one. Every time the cycle happened, we chipped a little more from our marriage. We could see it happening but did not break the cycle. I'm not sure which one of us finally waved the white flag, but we both knew it needed to happen. We could not go on that way and expect our marriage to survive. I don't think it was hard for us to admit we had a problem—that was pretty evident. Our issue was that each of us needed to do a real heart search with God and admit our own part in the problem. It's so much easier to point a finger at the other person than at yourself. With God's help we began to be completely transparent and honest with ourselves and each other. That was huge for us. Now, at last, we not only had the problem on the table, but we also each admitted the part we had played in the problem. Finally, we had something to work with. What we learned was that there is no problem that the three of us—Nancy, me, and God— could not resolve.

Is there an important topic or a sensitive issue that the two of you are ignoring? What obstacles keep you from dealing with it? What are potential consequences if you don't address it together? What is your first step?

## MARRIAGE IS A TEAM SPORT

Looking back, I wish I'd been as good an athlete as I thought I was. If I had been, there would be an Olympic gold medal hanging somewhere in my home. There's not. There are a few medals, but nothing even close to the Olympics. Nonetheless, track and cross-country taught me a lot. I learned the essence of self-discipline and hard work, as well as the consequences of avoiding them. I learned the importance of training with other people. They challenged and encouraged me. I learned the importance of a coach who believed in me. Without his wisdom, encouragement, and toughness, I would not have improved. Even though we were called the track team or the cross-country team, on game day, it was me against the world. Sure, my teammates and coach cheered for me and encouraged me, but at the end of the race it was just me. I either won or lost, and there was no one to point the finger at but me. Train together, prepare together, and then race alone. It was a love/hate deal for me.

By the time I met Nancy, my track and cross-country days were over. She knew of those days only from my stories, which I'm sure were much better than my actual accomplishments. Those years influenced me in several ways, but I never thought they would affect my marriage.

First, let's take a look at the positive impact. Marriage is sometimes compared to a marathon. It is a long race. To compete in long-distance running, I learned hard work and self-discipline. Those are two of the essentials that go into an awesome marriage. Marriage is work. Period. But just like winning a race, the hard work pays off. My nature is to be selfish and look out for myself first. It doesn't help to live in a culture that says it's okay to put myself first. It isn't okay—certainly not if you want a good marriage. Self-discipline helps me be unselfish. I can tell myself no when I need to. I can sacrifice myself for others.

In marriage, I have the best teammate imaginable. Nancy was designed to perfectly complement, challenge, and encourage me. From the day we said "I do," we are a team. Scripture tells us that life is better with two; if one falls down, the other can help them up (see Eccles. 4:9–10). Looking back, I cannot imagine what my life would be without her. Then there is our Coach. Neither of us can imagine our lives or marriage without Him. God has always been there for us. He gives us His wisdom, encouragement, and guidance. He has been there through everything.

I'm so thankful to have these realities in my marriage. My prayers were answered. Even so, sometimes in the reality of the marriage "race," something changes. Maybe it is the stress of life or minor irritations, but I can go from being Nancy's teammate with this amazing Coach to operating like a solitary person running against the world. My teammate becomes my enemy and I quit listening to my Coach. I go from the idea that marriage is a team sport to thinking that I don't need anyone and I can do it all on my own. And for a brief moment, I feel justified in that. Then, once again, I realize that will not work. I was not designed to be a one-man team—God blessed me with much more than that.

Today, I don't do that very often, if at all. With God's help I will stay on my team and value it as much as He does. What about you? Do you see your spouse as your marriage teammate? Can you see God as your Coach? The bottom line is that marriage is a team sport and life is better on the team.

## BEST FRIENDS OR BEST ENEMIES

What are some of the issues that can take you and your spouse from one type of "bestie" to the other? What can take us from being best friends to being best enemies? Let's look at three issues.

Benjamin and Charlotte were best friends. They dated in high school, then went their separate ways in college. They kept in touch, and then dated again in their late twenties. Both grew up in a suburb of Oklahoma City and went to the same schools since preschool. Charlotte went to the University of Oklahoma while Benjamin went out of state. Surprisingly, both wanted careers in advertising. During her senior year, Charlotte interned at a firm in Oklahoma City. After graduation, she was offered a position and began what turned out to be a very successful career. Benjamin's path was similar, and he took a position where he had interned for the summer before his senior year. Six years into their careers, a position opened in Charlotte's company that she felt Benjamin would be perfect for. He had mentioned more than once that he would like to return to Oklahoma City someday. Benjamin jumped at the opportunity, and six months later, he had an office just down the hall from Charlotte's. They were excited to spend time together but did not officially begin dating for about a year. Then things moved fast—less than a year later they were married.

During premarital counseling, they talked about whether they wanted to have children and how they would handle that step. They agreed that they wanted children, and both wanted Charlotte to be able to stay at home, at least until the children were in school. A couple of years later, Charlotte was pregnant. After the baby was born, she stayed at home. She loved being a mom but missed the job and company. Benjamin received a promotion and was on a steady path to becoming the second man in the company. That promotion came a couple of years later, and even though Charlotte was excited for him, there was a feeling of envy deep inside of her. Where did that come from? In the second year of Charlotte's time with the company, the president had come into her office one day. He lavished compliments on her work and as he left said, "You could certainly be my vice president someday."

Life had taken some different turns for her, and now the job she had dreamed of landed in Benjamin's lap. There was a special dinner to honor Benjamin and to formally announce his promotion. As Charlotte sat at the table, she was angry. Benjamin knew it. Since the news of the promotion, Charlotte had been distant and even cold to him at times. He wondered if she was jealous. She was, but Charlotte could not say those words. It sounded so petty. Instead of dealing with her feelings, she kept them inside, but they came out in a number of unhealthy ways.

Have you ever been jealous of your spouse's success? Sometimes it is difficult to stand in the shadows when your spouse is in the spotlight. Yet part of being a team is rejoicing with each other's success. It is a problem that I have seen manifest in many different ways in marriages. If it is an issue for you, don't keep it inside like Charlotte did. Get it out and begin to deal with yourself, your spouse, and God.

There is another issue that seems to confront many marriages. Sometimes one spouse sets aside their dreams so that the other can live theirs. Ethan and Olivia had been married about three years. Olivia had a knack for making jewelry. I guess it was more than a knack—it was a gift. People were amazed at the things she made. What began as a hobby and a way to make gifts for close friends and family gradually turned into a part-time business. Olivia was elated because people were actually willing to pay money for her products. Each year the demand grew. Olivia worked out of her house but now had a couple of other women helping her. She raised her prices twice, but sales continued to increase. One day a friend in commercial real estate called about a retail space opening in a local shopping center. With the mix of other tenants, Olivia's jewelry store would be a perfect fit. She couldn't wait to talk to Ethan about the idea. Ethan was happy for her and very supportive, though he knew his plans would have to be put on hold for a time. Ethan wanted to go to school to increase his computer knowledge. They had set money aside for that, but Ethan was more than willing to use it so that Olivia could open her store.

The store opened in the fall and was an instant success. Everyone seemed to know about Olivia's jewelry, and word of the new store spread fast. Olivia was a natural. She was not only creative with new jewelry designs but also great with customers. She gave mini seminars on fashion and using jewelry to define a look. Women were crazy about the store, and husbands now had a foolproof place to find a gift their wife was sure to love. Ethan became the backbone of the store. His computer knowledge was invaluable. He designed special programs to meet the store's needs and developed their online store.

The store doubled in its second year, and showed amazing increases each succeeding year. Each year Ethan thought about his dream of studying computers and eventually having his own company, but those dreams were stuffed. Little by little the resentment built, until one day Ethan sat in my office to talk it through. We met off and on for a few months. As we worked through some things, Ethan was able to see that God really had answered his prayer, just differently than he had expected. Ethan wanted his own business. He wanted to work with computers, be creative, and help companies build their businesses. He was doing all of those things. The store had always been in both of their names legally, even though Olivia's name was on the storefront. Ethan had probably learned more during their five years of business on the job than he would have in studying computers. Olivia always praised him and told everyone that Ethan was the reason for the store's success. Ethan saw that the enemy had distorted the truth and blinded him to the realities in front of him. God had done exceedingly more than Ethan ever asked for or dreamed of.

Has God ever done that for you? Has He answered a prayer very differently than you thought He would, yet in a way that was much better for you? Don't be deceived into thinking God doesn't hear your prayers. He does. He will never do anything less than what's best for you, your spouse, and your marriage.

## ANGER AND MARRIAGE

We all get angry. Jesus got angry. Being angry is an emotion just like being happy, sad, or ecstatic. When handled the wrong way, anger has a tendency to tear marriages apart. The Bible tells us to "be angry and do not sin." What does that mean? It means that if I am angry at Nancy, I have a choice of how to react. If I yell at her, throw something at her, or hit her, I have sinned. If I say in a controlled way, "I'm really angry and we need to talk this through," I have not sinned. See the difference?

In life and in marriage, anger is a red flag that lets us

know something is wrong. *Then* we have a choice. This is where most of us get off base. We don't realize we have a choice in our behavior, thus we say things like, "I hit him because he made me mad." No, you didn't. You hit him because you chose to do so. Example: Aiden and Avery are having an argument. Avery is standing her ground and fighting back verbally. It makes Aiden more and more mad. Avery has decided that this time she will not back down or let Aiden overpower her with his words. Finally, in anger and frustration, Aiden shoves her and she falls backward on the floor.

Aiden tells me the following week that Avery made him shove her. He doesn't see that he made a choice. Granted, the choice happened very quickly, but it happened. I ask him, "If Jesus was in the room watching the fight, would you have shoved Avery?"

His answer: "No!"

"If you could make the choice *not to*, you made a choice *to*."

Anger is not a sin. How we handle anger determines whether it is sin or not. Aiden sinned when he shoved Avery. When we act out our anger, we change our marriage relationship from "friend" to "foe." That takes us in the opposite direction of an awesome marriage.

Nancy and I were married five years before we had kids. We needed every bit of those five years plus a few more to figure out our lives together. Both of us would say that we seldom, if ever, argued with someone in a previous relationship. I never remember getting mad at anyone I ever

dated (not that my list was very long), so it was somewhat
of a shock that we both became instant fighting experts.
Our fights made me think that there was no way at all we
would ever make it. Nancy would dig in her heels and so
would I. There was no way we were giving in to the other,
so this became our cycle. We would fight. We would yell
and scream and not listen to a word the other was saying.
The louder we yelled, the madder we got, and the less we
heard. Each was waiting for something that was never going to happen—for the other person to back down. Finally,
we would stop yelling and not speak to each other for a
day or so. Then we would begin to feel bad and kind of
miss each other and tell each other we were sorry. We had a
"honeymoon" period. We talked again, had fun, made love,
but never resolved anything. The good period could last a
few days, weeks, or sometimes even a few months, but the
cycle always continued.

This is what I observed. Even though the honeymoon
periods could be good, the fights got worse and tore a little
more at our marriage every time they happened. From the
friend versus foe standpoint, the friendship always eroded a
little more, and that erosion settled on the foe side of the
relationship. If it had not stopped, we would not have made
it. Nobody gets married to have someone to fight with for
the next fifty years. Right?

Finally, we realized we were killing our relationship.
When we were not fighting, we valued the relationship
a lot. We had to learn how to resolve conflict or we
would continue the cycle over and over again. Probably

the biggest help for us was learning how to listen to each other. When Nancy was talking, I needed to listen to her so that I understood what she was saying and respond in a way that let her know I heard her. If I listened and did not understand, I needed to ask her to say it again until I got it. The same went for her. You know what was really cool? Probably at least 90 percent of the time, simply understanding each other solved the problem. So many of our arguments and fights came from misunderstanding or making assumptions about each other. With those off the table, there was little to fight about. Do you relate to the anger/honeymoon cycle? Are there issues that you never seem to resolve as a couple? What about starting to really listen to each other?

## WHO ARE YOU?

There is one other area I think many couples are vulnerable to. It involves issues with the opposite sex that originated with previous relationships. If you were in a relationship where you felt controlled by the other person, you may be ultra sensitive to anything that even hints of control. You may think your spouse is trying to control you when that is not their intent at all. Many of us have been in relationships in which we could not trust the other person. Your spouse may have never done anything to cause mistrust, but because of a past relationship you are constantly on guard and suspicious.

Then there is the baggage that we can all bring into a marriage. It can be from our family of origin or from a previous relationship or life experience. When we bring baggage and do not deal with it, it will keep affecting not only us but also our marriage. There is physical abuse and sexual abuse, and lying and infidelity; there are all kinds of mistrust. I see many people who have been affected by one or more of these. When the issue is dealt with and healing begins to take place, the effect on a marriage can be minimal. If not dealt with, these can be ruinous to a marriage.

Emily was twelve when her parents divorced. She knew their marriage was not very good because she often heard them fighting. What she did not know was that her dad was having an affair. Apparently, he told her mom over and over that the affair was done and he was going to be faithful, but it wasn't. Finally, Emily's mom had enough. Her dad moved out. Her mom told Emily far more than she needed to know. Emily's dad told her that nothing would change and that she would see him just as much as ever. That also turned out to be a lie.

Emily thought, *My dad seems to be good at lying. Maybe all men lie.* At twelve, that made sense to her. It was just a few weeks later when Emily figured out that her dad was living with another woman with two kids, ages eight and four. By the end of the year, Emily felt her dad had left her just like he had left her mom. Emily never said that to anyone but she knew it was true. She could not trust him and probably not any other man either. Through high school Emily had only one date even though she was popular and got asked out a lot. She attended the senior prom with the literal boy next door, who was like a brother. That was safe.

After high school, Emily worked at a local bank and took some night classes. She really liked banking and enjoyed the people she worked with. Logan also worked at the bank. He seemed nice, and they gradually became friends. It was over a year before he asked her out. She surprised herself by saying yes, before she realized what that meant for her. Over the months of dating, she began to think that Logan might be okay. Maybe he was not like her dad or the other men. When he asked her to marry him, again she said yes. Their wedding was small. Emily didn't want to have to deal with the whole "Dad is supposed to give you away" thing. They honeymooned in Mexico and came back to begin their life together.

I saw Emily's mom after her divorce and knew Emily from that time on. I never counseled Emily because she always said she was "fine." Her mom never pushed it. Then Emily and Logan celebrated their first anniversary. The following week Emily was in my office. She knew she loved Logan but did not know why was she so afraid that he was being unfaithful to her. There was no real evidence, but the way he acted reminded her of her dad when she was twelve. Emily had never mentioned any of this to Logan. I asked her to bring him with her to the next appointment. As we sat together, Emily shared with Logan what she had shared with me the week before. I could not have scripted Logan's response any better than he did. He affirmed his love, promised his faithfulness, and then looked puzzled over the things he did that reminded her of her dad. Logan helped Emily understand that what she saw and what he meant were totally different than what she saw in her dad. Emily continued counseling to work on the issues that were now on the table. Logan went above and beyond in being accountable and filling every gap he could to show his faithfulness to her. With God's help, Emily was able to see the lies that she had believed about men for a long time. Sure, there were other men like her dad, but Logan was not one of them. Then the big turnaround happened. Emily forgave her dad. Today Logan and Emily have a great marriage. They are on the same team—not foes.

## KEYS TO DEALING WITH CONFLICT

As we complete this chapter, here are some things I want you to think about:

- When we talked about issues or topics that get swept under the rug, did anything come to mind from your marriage? If so, are you ready to deal with it now?
- Is there anything that is keeping you as a couple from being a team and embracing God as your Coach? What is it? Are you willing to work on it together?
- Have you ever been jealous in any way of your spouse's success? When was that? Have you shared that with your spouse so that you can begin to deal with it together? Will you do that now?

- We all have dreams for our lives, and life often takes a different direction. Has that happened to you? Take time to see what God is doing with that dream.
- If I had you rate your anger on a scale of one to ten, with ten being rage, where would your rating fall? Is anger a problem for you? In your own words, how does the principle "be angry and do not sin" apply to you?
- Have you ever looked at your spouse and seen someone from a previous damaging relationship? Pray that God will help you see your spouse as who they are, not as someone else.

---

*Going Deeper*

Seeing your spouse as the enemy is a sure path toward your marriage ending in a train wreck. Seeing your spouse as your friend is a sure way to be on the same team. Write out three lies you have believed about your spouse that have led you to look at them as an enemy. Pray that God will heal you from the lies you've believed. Write out three truths about your spouse as your friend who fights with you for your marriage. Pray that God will embed these truths in your marriage.

# CHAPTER 7

---

# Mammon and God: Money and Spirituality

The Bible has a lot to say about living in a way that fulfills us and glorifies God. For me, it's kind of like a road map. When I follow the map, life is pretty good. I don't create as many problems for myself and others, and I never feel alone. When I get off the map or leave it behind, I easily get lost, and life is much more complicated. It's like losing my compass on a dark, cloudy night. I lose sight of where I am and I'm not sure which direction to go.

Does the Bible talk about everything? No. If I need a hammer, I don't go to the Bible; I go to Home Depot. What the Bible does teach me is how to act toward other drivers on my way to the store and how to treat the employees when I get there. It teaches me to pay for the hammer instead of stealing it. The Bible helps me become more of who God designed me to be with over five hundred verses on prayer and almost five hundred verses on faith. Then there is one topic that is mentioned over two thousand times in the Bible. It comprised over 15 percent of all that

Jesus taught about. It's the most mentioned topic in the Bible: money.

Why money over prayer, faith, sin, or salvation? I don't think that is an accident. I think, like everything else God does, it is very intentional. Of all the things God could teach us, He chose to put more emphasis on money than anything else. That alone should tell us something. Is money evil? Are we doomed if we have money? Should we give it all away? Here's my take on money. First, money is a good gift from God. It allows us to provide for our family and to help others. In our world, money, for most of us, is a part of day-to-day existence. Second, money can be a temptation because it seems as though it could deliver everything that we want or desire. Money then becomes the key to happiness. The problem, though, does not lie with money; it lies with us.

In the movie *All the Money in the World*, multibillionaire J. Paul Getty is asked how much money is enough. His answer speaks volumes: "More." "More" is the problem with us and money. We believe the lie that more money will bring more happiness, more security, more freedom. Yet, if we look at many of the lives of those with "more," we see those promises are false. Money does not make a good god. Jesus tells us, "You can't worship two gods at once. Loving one god, you'll end up hating the other. Adoration of one feeds contempt for the other. You can't worship God and Money both" (Matt. 6:24 MSG). I think most of us can logically get there. We can agree that money does not bring all those things that we want to believe it can bring. But living day to day, we certainly have the tendency to fall back into the trap of thinking money is the answer.

Let's go back to my point that money is a good gift from God. Money and mammon are different. Oxford's online dictionary defines "mammon" this way: "Wealth regarded as an evil influence or false object of worship and devotion." That's where we get into trouble. Mammon gets in the way of our relationship with God, our spouse, and most other things that we would say are of importance to us. Money is like other gifts from God that we distort. For example, sex is an incredible gift of God to be enjoyed in marriage, but our culture has distorted sex to the point that it is a source of sadness and pain for many people.

So is our next step to sell everything and give it all away? No. Our next step is to look at money through God's eyes and to use it as the gift He has given us. For most of us, this will be an ongoing process because culture screams the money message very loudly. Let's look at money from the perspective of relationships: God and marriage.

## MONEY SECRETS

Don't get too excited. This is not about a secret formula to get more money. Instead let's look at how keeping money secrets separates a couple in marriage. Here are some questions to ask yourself:

- As a couple, do I keep my money separate?

- Do I have a credit card that my spouse does not know about?
- Do I hide purchases from my spouse?

If you answer yes to any of the above, keep reading. In fact, even if you did not answer yes to any of the above, keep reading. I want to help you make sure you never say yes to any of them.

I'm not for separation in any area of marriage. That's not how marriage was designed. If you want to be separate, why did you get married? There are a number of couples that will fight against separation in almost every area of their marriage, except money. Money seems to be the sacred cow of many marriages. "You can have all of me but not my money." And therein lies the problem—"my money." That is not a bank issue; it is a heart issue.

Let me unpack this with you. As a Christian, I believe that everything I have comes from God. Sure, I work and earn money, but the ability to work and the skills I have essentially came to me from God. So I look at money in the same way. Everything is God's. He is the owner. He has entrusted me with some of His estate—money. My role is to manage well what I have. I see principles in the Bible that encourage me to provide for my family and to be generous. God gives me a lot of flexibility with the money He has given me. I don't see Him looking over my shoulder every time I make a purchase. It goes back to the heart. If I seek God and live my life each day in a way that honors Him, love my wife and family to the best of my ability, then most likely, my heart will be in the right place. If I do not seek God and I put myself in first place above all else, my heart will not be in the right place, and my selfishness will rule. I have a choice every day. When my heart is right, money is just money and in marriage it is "our money." When my heart is not right, money becomes mammon.

Putting our money together was never an issue for us, partly because we got married so young. In college, we both had individual bank accounts, but honestly, other than some money from summer jobs, we were funded by our parents. For me the "funding" stopped when I graduated and began a full-time job, which was only for six months before Nancy and I married. Plus I lived at home. When we married, Nancy was in her junior year and had not been on her own. It was easy for us to put almost nothing together! We had one bank account and one checkbook. I worked. She finished school. (Her parents still covered tuition.) It was "our money" from day one and always has been that way. Chalk up one thing we did right from the beginning!

Today, there are other couples in our shoes who marry early and share money from the moment they say "I do." The majority of the couples I see have different stories. Many marry later in life after both have started jobs or careers and have been doing life on their own for a while. Many have lived on their own for years. The separation has been established and they are often reluctant to handle money differently. Other couples have been in a long-term relationship or previous marriage where money was a real issue for one reason or another. They trusted someone with "their money" once and are not eager to do that again.

This is what I say to all couples concerning money. I really don't care if you have one account, two, or however many. I don't care if you have one checkbook or two or ten! What I do care about is your marriage and the separation that money can bring. If you see all you have as yours together, then the practicalities of bank accounts and checkbooks are a personal preference. Both people need to be involved in the money. Both need to know what the expenses are. Both need to follow the budget. Both need to be totally open with each other concerning money. When you put God first and your spouse second, how you handle the money will fall into place. If you don't, you will be one of the many couples who say money is the number one problem in their marriage. Which do you want to be? How do you look at money in your marriage today? Do you trust each other as far as money? Depending on your answers to these questions, what is your next step with money and your marriage?

Noah and Aubrey had separate bank accounts. When the bills came in, Noah wrote a check for 65 percent and Aubrey wrote a check for 35 percent of each bill. Michael and Zoey had been married three years. Zoey had two credit cards that Michael did not know existed. Carter and Hannah had a budget. Hannah had a certain amount of money each week to spend on groceries and other expenses. Hannah discovered that she could manipulate the money and make purchases for herself that Carter did not know about. All three marriages were heading for disaster. The only variable was when.

Aubrey was never completely on board with the percentage system Noah came up with for their bills. Noah thought it made sense because he brought in 65 percent of the income while Aubrey brought in 35 percent. It just did not seem right. Her dream was a husband who could and would provide for her. Sure, she worked and liked her work. That was not the problem. She just did not feel the security she wanted from her marriage. As time went on, the percentage system affected their marriage in different ways. Aubrey wanted some new furniture for their home. Most of their furniture was from early marriage, garage sales, or hand-me-downs. Noah, on the other hand, wanted a sound system for the home. They sat down to discuss what they would do, but from the beginning Noah's mind was made up. In his mind, it was going to be the sound system because his vote carried more weight. After all, he brought in more money than she did. That was really the beginning of the end of the marriage for Aubrey. The separation of their money was bleeding all over the rest of their marriage.

Zoey knew that money would be tight in the first years of marriage. Michael was finishing training for his job while working full-time. Zoey had a job she loved, but it wasn't the best-paying job around. With Michael's schedule, they decided Zoey would pay the bills. They were both going to be involved in the money, but over time, Michael's involvement faded. They decided together to stick to their budget, which was tight but doable. A year after Zoey and Michael's wedding, Zoey's sister got married. Her husband was doing well in his job and she worked three days a week as a nurse. Every time Zoey went to her sister's home, she saw something else she wished she had for her home. She noticed her sister always had new clothes. One day a credit card application came in the mail. It said Zoey was pre-approved. Why not send it in and see what would happen?

A couple of weeks later Zoey had a credit card in her own name, and Michael had no idea. She started by buying a few little things for herself that she knew Michael would not notice. The little purchases turned into bigger purchases. She finally bought the table she wanted for their living room. She lied and told Michael a friend who was moving gave it to her. The pattern of lying and buying continued. The practice of paying off the card each month ended, and Zoey got another card as the first one was maxed out. Michael just happened to come home for lunch one day as the mail arrived. In the mail was a letter addressed to Zoey that looked like a bill. He took it with him and confronted Zoey that evening. She burst into tears and confessed about the cards. The two balances that Michael did not even know existed totaled almost seven thousand dollars. He left the house with no idea how they would pay this off or how he could ever trust Zoey again. He wondered who she really was.

Hannah and Carter took the marriage prep course that I teach. They also took a finance course together and felt they were well prepared to keep money from being an issue in their marriage. They agreed on a budget and that Hannah would be the one to write the checks. They would look over the budget together every month. Hannah wasn't sure when she had "juggled the books" for the first time. She just knew there was extra in the grocery budget and that she used it to buy something she wanted without telling Carter. Looking back, the funny thing was that Carter would have said, "Sure, buy it," if she had asked.

The pattern of shifting money continued, and Hannah kept her purchases secret from Carter. When they looked at the budget each month, everything looked great because it never told the real story. The problem escalated when Carter brought up the idea of cutting a few things back to start a savings account. They adjusted the budget and put a line in for savings. Hannah told herself that her days of manipulating the budget were over, but that did not last long. She knew that Carter would eventually find out about everything. The "savings" line in the budget was getting larger with nothing to back it up. When it reached fifteen hundred dollars, Carter thought they should invest part of it to try to get a larger return on their investment. In tears, Hannah confessed the truth. Carter was devastated. He never in a million years thought Hannah could do something like that. He asked himself, "Now what do I do?"

I could tell you many more stories of money and marriage. You probably could too. Find any list of "problems in marriage" and you will find money at or near the top of the list. It seems in every story that I can think of there was the transition of money into mammon. Money was never the problem. It was the heart that made the trans-formation. If money was just something God gave us to help navigate marriage and we kept it in that perspective, these stories wouldn't exist. People don't come to counsel-ing to tell me about their success with their budget. They do come to counseling to talk about mammon. When a spouse uses money to get their way, hides money from the other, acquires secret credit cards, hides purchases or covers them by manipulating the budget, there is a problem. A big problem.

My experience tells me that more people fight over money spent than money saved. Fights about money spent involve how much is spent, why it was spent, why it was charged, why the account is overdrawn again, why the bills can't be paid, etc. A fight about money saved is really about money not saved and the fear that we have nothing to fall back on if something happens. The fighting can vary in intensity with a lot hinging on the personalities and frustra-tion level of those involved.

If there were do-overs available, would Noah, Zoey, and Hannah jump at the chance? I think so. Their marriages were in shambles. Two of the three couples made it, but it took a long time and a lot of building. God showed up big-time in these couples' lives. God was showing up in the other marriage, too, but somebody closed the door. When you hear these three stories, what comes to your mind? Have you been tempted to do the same? Have you crossed that line? Has your spouse crossed the line? My best counsel is to never cross the line, but if you already have, know that we have a God who can heal anything and can turn mammon back into money!

## MONEY SPENT

As much as most of us think that budgets are a good idea, the research says only about a third of us follow through. I think there is a fear that our spouse might use the budget as a tool to control or manipulate us. Then I think some of us don't want to put in the effort to create and keep up with a budget, even though there are programs and apps that do practically everything for us. Think about this. I have never talked to a couple who regretted creating and following a budget. In fact, they say it is one of the best decisions they made as a couple. More than half of these couples used to fight about money every single month. Having and following a budget will not guarantee zero fights over money, but it will come close. You know how much comes in and how much goes out. You know that if less comes in than goes out, you have to make some changes. You know if there is more income than expenses, you have extra. The biggest benefit that I see with a budget is that if you create it and agree on it together, you have made a big step away from separation in your marriage.

John and Leah fought over money, beginning when they were dating. Leah could never understand why John spent money on his hobby when he could have saved instead. John would buy a nice surprise gift for Leah, and she would ruin the moment by asking how much it cost and berating John for spending "that kind of money." Would it surprise you that the reason they came to counseling soon after their marriage was money? I asked them what turned out to be a rhetorical question. "Did you not see the danger signs with the two of you and money before you married?" John answered for the two of them, "Yes, but we thought it would just work out in marriage." Let me tell you something. Nothing just works itself out in marriage!

So there they sat. A spender and a saver. John was not what I would call a big spender. He had his hobby and he liked to buy gifts for people, but he never went outside of his budget in doing so. If you were to draw an arrow on a picture pointing to a saver, Leah would be at the far tip of the arrow. I would probably change her classification from "saver" to "miser." How in the world had these two people fallen in love and made it this far? My common ground with them was their faith. Leah could practically quote every Scripture that warned about the hazards of money. In her book, money was evil. There were other positives going for them. They really did love each other and they wanted to figure this out. I outlined my game plan for them:

- Both of you are going to have to give some.
- There is a difference between money and mammon. Money is not evil.
- Continuing to be separate with money will never work for you long-term.
- A budget could really help your situation.

- In your budget, each could have discretionary money to spend however you choose. (I knew right away that Leah would be saving all of hers.)
- Pray. Pray for God to unite you in this separateness of money.

I never expected a miracle with them and, while that miracle did not come, step-by-step they came together. John could not wait to tell me about when he brought home a small gift for Leah and her response was, "Thank you!" For them, that might have been a miracle.

## MONEY SAVED

According to a 2017 CNN report, most Americans have less than five hundred dollars in savings. That can cause stress in a marriage. Having no emergency fund when there is an emergency will cause problems. Where will the money come from? If a couple reaches retirement age with nothing saved, that causes more problems. It means one or both will have to continue to work, lower their standard of living, move in with their kids, or do something else that they would rather not have to do. In either case, a couple can point fingers at each other and place blame. Having no money there when it is needed can cause big issues in a marriage. Having an emergency fund and planning for retirement make a difference in the money stress level in a marriage.

I also know many couples end up in a bad financial situation through no real fault of their own. The economy can turn, a job can be unexpectedly terminated, or there can be an illness that literally drains the bank account. There is no way we can anticipate the future, but there are some steps that will help us if things go bad.

- First, pray for God's wisdom with your finances.
- Second, decide together to save. Get on the same team here and stay on the same team.
- Third, if you are in debt, start a plan to get out. If a crisis comes, being debt-free can make a big difference.
- Fourth, start saving. Get your emergency fund, then start saving for the future. It is not too late, and if you are young, you will never look back and regret that you were very intentional with your money.

As a couple, how would you respond to that CNN survey? Are you in the group with less than five hundred dollars in savings, or are you making good choices? Have you been putting off saving? Are you living like the debt is not there? You will feel a big weight lifted simply by making the decision to address your financial future together.

### NATALIE AND JOSEPH

Natalie and Joseph were the youngest couple I ever counseled who had been forced into bankruptcy. Joseph was twenty-four and Natalie was twenty-three. Joseph was brilliant. He developed software that could make him a lot of money, and it did. When Joseph told me that he felt "bulletproof," I knew exactly what he meant. There were a lot of things I loved about my early twenties, and feeling bulletproof was one of them. The money was coming in, and he and Natalie were living a life they had never dreamed of. A big house in an exclusive gated community. Three really cool cars for the two of them to drive. Trips on private planes. Opportunities to invest in other start-up companies. Things were good—too good. Joseph told me that it took only about six months for his "empire" to come crashing down. All the people that were there for him one day disappeared the next. It was Joseph and Natalie against the world. He fought against bankruptcy until the attorney he trusted said he had no choice. That was the Joseph I met that day. All the material possessions were gone, but he still had the most important thing in his life. Natalie sat by his side.

The first question this brilliant young man who went from the mountaintop to the valley asked me was, "What do you think God wants me to learn?" For the next six months we talked about some other practical day-to-day things for their marriage, but the primary focus was on answering that question. Joseph knew that if he learned what God wanted him to learn, he would not repeat the same mistakes. He knew he would commit new mistakes but not the same old ones. I'm not going to tell you what happened to Joseph and Natalie over the next few years because that is not the point. I will tell you that because they sought God and His wisdom,

God showed up, and He will do the same for you and for me. Are you learning from your mistakes? Are you seeking God's wisdom? If we learn from our mistakes, then nothing is lost. What does God want you to learn?

## KEYS TO DEALING WITH MONEY

As we complete this chapter, here are some things I want you to think about:

- Where are you with money? Is it *money* or *mammon*?
- Is money separating the two of you, or do you handle it in a way that unites you?
- Do you ever hide a credit card or purchases from your spouse?
- When it comes to money, what do you fight over?
- If CNN did a new survey on saving money, how would you respond?
- Do you seek God's wisdom with your money and how to use it?
- Depending on how you answered the above questions, what is your next step?

---

### Going Deeper

Talking about money and what to do with it can be a far stretch from actually taking action. Pray for God's wisdom and together come up with three things you can agree on as a couple that will lead you to financial freedom in your marriage. That's your game plan.

There is only one topic in the Bible where God says, "Test me." Guess what it has to do with? If you said money, you're right. In Malachi 3:10, God talks about generosity and bringing tithes to the church and then says, "If you do, I will open the windows of heaven for you. I will pour out a blessing so great you won't have enough room to take it in! Try it! Put me to the test" (NLT). If you have never taken this challenge, what are you waiting for?

# CHAPTER 8

# Friendship: Who Is Your "Bestie"?

### WHAT ARE YOU LOOKING FOR?

Sometime in my middle school years, I made a startling discovery about friendship. Not all friends are equal. That may not seem like some great revelation to you, but at that time in my life, it was huge. Before that, I looked at all friendships the same. I trusted everyone and made no distinction in what I told one person or another. I had never been betrayed (as far as I knew). I treated everyone the same and felt that was reciprocated. When someone asked me who my best friend was, I would hesitate because I looked at every friend as a best friend. Then in eighth grade Billy Hudson entered my life. Billy was new to our school that year but we treated him like he had been there forever. I never really questioned whether I could trust Billy or not; I just did.

One weekend he spent the night at my house. He asked

me a lot of questions, but I really did not think it was
strange since Billy was the new kid. He asked me about
girls and who I liked and I told him—something I had never
told anyone before. I was nowhere close to wanting a girl
I liked to know that I liked her. By the time I got to second hour on Monday morning back at school, everyone
knew I liked Elina Harper. Guess who was in my second-
hour class? I thought I was going to die. I went to the office,
called my mom, and told her I was really sick (which was
not a big stretch) and needed to come home. As I lay in my
bed at home that afternoon, I had no idea if I could ever
trust anyone again. For a boy in eighth grade, that was a
tough lesson to learn. Not everyone is trustworthy, and the
number of people I could really trust shrank that day to
about four.

What do you look for in a best friend? What's essential?
What's not? What do you expect from a best friend?
Suzanne Degges-White is a licensed counselor and pro-
fessor at Northern Illinois University. In an online article
for *Psychology Today*, Degges-White lists thirteen essential
friendship traits. She lists the traits in the first person, but I
am adjusting that to fit what we are talking about. Here are
thirteen qualities of a best friend:

1. Someone trustworthy
2. Someone who is honest with you
3. Someone who is generally very dependable
4. Someone who is loyal to the people they care about
5. Someone who is easily able to trust others

6. Someone who experiences and expresses empathy for others
7. Someone who is able to be non-judgmental
8. Someone who is a good listener
9. Someone who is supportive of others in their good times
10. Someone who is supportive of others in their bad times
11. Someone who is self-confident
12. Someone who is usually able to see the humor in life
13. Someone who is fun to be around

Is that what you are looking for in a best friend? Does that cover it for you? Is there anything you would add? Anything that you would take away? I like the list. In fact, when I saw it, I didn't think I could come up with anything better. Now you have a checklist for best friends. When you meet someone who has potential, you can begin to check off the qualities you see in them. If they are thirteen for thirteen, they are in. Anything less than thirteen is your call, but if you find someone who bats one thousand as a friend every day, let me know.

Now let's look at the list as Dr. Degges-White originally wrote it.

1. I am trustworthy.
2. I am honest with others.
3. I am generally very dependable.
4. I am loyal to the people I care about.
5. I am easily able to trust others.

6. I experience and express empathy for others.
7. I am able to be non-judgmental.
8. I am a good listener.
9. I am supportive of others in their good times.
10. I am supportive of others in their bad times.
11. I am self-confident.
12. I am usually able to see the humor in life.
13. I am fun to be around.

I think we all know that friendship is a two-way street, but it is also easy to forget our role. It's easy to point the finger when a friend lets us down, doesn't listen when we want them to, or just isn't in the mood for fun when we are. I have to ask myself, how consistent am I in fulfilling the list? How would a friend grade me? What about you?

All of this is foundational to friendship in marriage. If other friendships have gone wrong in the past, we can be skeptical or reluctant to fully trust our spouse. If past friendships have been good, it usually will be easier to see our spouse in the same way. As I look through the list, I can sometimes look at it as a to-do list for Nancy, but do I also make it a to-do list for me? Don't get me wrong. You are not going to be perfect and neither is your spouse, but if you are consistently trying to be a best friend day after day, you are definitely on the right track. Your spouse will see your heart. I want Nancy and me to have this kind of friendship. I want all of those qualities knit into the fabric of our marriage. I want her to be my best friend today, tomorrow, and all the tomorrows after that—and I want to be hers. Is it easy? No. It takes work just like other friendships. The difference is that in marriage the benefits are greater than any other friendship could ever be. That's worth all the effort. Isn't that what you are looking for?

## GRACE AND MASON

When I talk to couples as they prepare for marriage, we talk about all the reasons they want to spend the rest of their lives together. The term "best friends" inevitably turns up. It did for Nancy and me. We were best friends going into marriage, and being best friends helped us as we weathered some marriage storms. It came pretty easy for us. We were intentional without knowing it. Spending time together, talking, and listening all happened for us—and all three are foundational to a friendship.

Grace and Mason had been married over twenty years. Their story of friendship pretty much mirrored ours. They were both in their early twenties when they met in a church singles' program. The program grew, and the church decided that it was time to form small groups. Grace and Mason were asked to lead one of the small groups. It was during that year and a half that their friendship took off. They took leading the small group seriously and spent a lot of time together planning and preparing. They did not see each other as boyfriend and girlfriend, which was interesting looking back. The series they were doing in their small group was about defining the qualities to look for in a potential mate. Mason said it was after the rest of the group left that evening that he looked at Grace and realized she was everything he was looking for. So he told her. Unfortunately for Mason, Grace had not yet come to the same realization. He felt really stupid and made up some lame excuse that he was just joking. Grace knew better and although she had not thought of them as a couple before, it sparked something inside of her—in a really good way. Another eighteen months passed and these two best friends were now husband and wife. In talking to Grace and Mason, I was able to put some thoughts together about friendship and marriage.

First, a strong friendship as the foundation of a marriage can make a significant difference when hard times come. Grace talked about some difficult things they went through as a couple. The first test was a miscarriage three years into marriage. As hard as that was, Grace said it strengthened their marriage. "I didn't want anyone but God and my best friend, and both were there for me." The same story played out for both of them as they lived out the years of their marriage. No matter what happened, they had each other. Not only was being best friends fun but they learned firsthand the depth of their friendship and how God used it in each of their lives day after day. Was their marriage always great? No, but through tears, anger, fears, and lots of other things, they always came back to one thing. Neither wanted to lose the other and the friendship they cherished. That friendship foundation was always there.

Second, it is important to value that friendship and not let anything into your life that would harm it in any way. Most of us know from experience that maintaining good friendships over time does not just happen. We have to continue doing the things that established and cemented the friendship in the first place. For friendship in marriage, take that up a few notches. Our expectations of our spouse are higher than other friendships, and rightly so. This is *the* relationship in this life. Nancy is my best friend. We worked on it in the beginning and we work on it today. There were times that we didn't do a good job. For us, it was letting life get in the way: good things like kids, work, volunteering, sports, hobbies, and other friends. If we were not intentional, any of those would take away more time from each other than was healthy for maintaining our friendship in marriage.

The good things that take away are the tricky ones. They sneak up on us a little at a time, and often we don't even notice the harm they are doing. Then there are things that are not healthy and kill friendships. This includes everything from drugs and alcohol to flirtations and affairs—you know the list. The bottom line is this: Anything that we let into our life that hurts our friendship with our spouse is dangerous. The fallout from these can have varying consequences. The best course of action? With the first group, keep things in balance. With the second group, don't!

Third, cherish and enjoy your friendship. A building friendship got us to the altar. It gave us something to work back to when we were distant because we valued it so much. It has given each of us someone to live life with who deeply cares. Plus, there is no one that I have more fun with than Nancy. Friendship in marriage is one of those special gifts that God gives us.

## THAT'S FUNNY

Laughing with your spouse is fun. Laughing at your spouse is not. Do you laugh together? Laughter knits a couple together in a unique way. It does something for a marriage that nothing else quite does. I try to make Nancy laugh every day. I love to see and hear her laugh. Her laugh makes me laugh. Laughter truly is a great medicine. There are a lot of things I love about being married as long as we have, and one of them is the history of laughter together. Funny things that happened years ago can still bring laughter when one of us brings the memories to mind. There are also those things we laugh about that no one else would ever get. We have had funny things happen during sex and when we were supposed to be quiet. Some of the things we laugh about today were not funny to both of us in the past. Time has a way of reframing things so that looking back gives us a different perspective.

There was the time I was getting ready to put something in the attic and could not get the pull-down ladder in the garage to come down. Nancy was standing there holding whatever it was that needed to go in the attic. Finally, I gave one final tug and the ladder came down, fast and with a lot of force. And even though I was running the opposite way, it knocked me to the garage floor. Nothing was hurt but my pride. Nancy could not help herself from laughing. I made it worse by being angry at the ladder, the garage, her, and whatever she was holding. Today I can visualize how I must have looked, and can laugh with her about the whole incident.

Recently our twelve-year-old grandson, Tommy, was spending the night. Nancy asked him what he wanted for dinner, and he said Asian food. To give you some background, Nancy and I have one favorite Asian restaurant that is our go-to for takeout. Tommy wanted something from a different restaurant about two blocks from our favorite. When it was time to go pick up the order, Nancy volunteered to go while Tommy and I were in a hot battle on Xbox One. My phone rang about fifteen minutes later, and I could tell from the sound of her voice that Nancy was a little frustrated. "What number did you put the order under? They can't find it." Our restaurant uses cell phone numbers to identify orders while the other restaurant, where our order was waiting for her, uses last names. I said, "You are at the wrong restaurant." After we hung up, I told Tommy what had happened, and the two of us were rolling on the floor with laughter. When Nancy finally got home with the order, neither of us said a thing. A couple of days later, Nancy and I were driving somewhere and I finally brought it up. At first, I thought I shouldn't have, but her attempt at a stoic look soon turned into a smile and plenty of laughter for both of us. I think we have learned to not take ourselves too seriously and to find humor wherever we can. Humor is a great bonding agent.

I'm not sure when or how it happens—the answer probably varies from couple to couple—but I see way too many couples who have somehow eliminated laughter from their marriage. It's like Scotty beamed it up. Almost every couple I know would say that humor was a part of their relationship at some time. Somewhere along their path of marriage it was lost. I think it often happens as a couple drifts apart and the things that once held them together drift away too.

Nancy and I were at a movie not very long ago. She went to the women's room before the movie began and I waited for her in the theater lobby. There was a guy sitting on a bench outside the women's room waiting for his date (not sure, but they looked like early marriage) to come out. He was holding one of those huge buckets of popcorn. About ten seconds before his date came out of the bathroom, he dropped the bucket. I mean dropped it to the ground with mounds of popcorn all around him. This is the cool part. As his wife walked out of the bathroom and her eyes landed on the scene, they both broke out in laughter. Then, everyone around who had witnessed the event laughed too. What would you have done if that was your spouse? What would your spouse have done? There are a lot of different endings to that story. What would yours have looked like?

## YOUR CHECKLIST

There have been many times in my life that I have created a checklist for something without realizing it. It's not like I sat down and made a list with little boxes beside each item. Instead, this checklist develops in my mind. Sometimes I am aware of it but just as often, I am not. Seeing Dr. Degges-

White's list that we talked about earlier in the chapter really helped me to realize that I had a "what I want from my wife as a best friend" list in my mind. Do you have this list of friendship qualities you want from your spouse? I discovered that I have probably had a checklist for our entire relationship. I think over time it has definitely changed some. Some things that were once a priority are still on the list but in a different position. There is nothing wrong with a checklist. What I have learned is that when it comes to a friendship checklist in marriage or any checklist in marriage, I have to make sure I am doing well the things that I want Nancy to do well. Think about that for a minute. It's not the way we usually look at checklists. If I have a checklist for someone, I write the list, and when they do what's on my list, I check off the box. That never has and never will work in marriage. Never!

Think through this with me. It has always been important to me that Nancy is trustworthy and honest. Probably because I saw these qualities in her and came to value them so much. Yet is it ever fair for me to expect her to be these while not embracing them as things I need to do for her? If you are even wavering in your answer, it is *no*! Not only is it not fair, it's not who God wants me to be as her husband. Here is my point for us. My checklist for friendship in marriage has to have two rows of boxes to check. Mine and hers. In fact, my checklist really needs to have only one row of boxes—they are for me, not for her. If I consistently do the things in my marriage to build and maintain and grow our friendship, that's what I am supposed to do. And, in our marriage, when I am consistent with these, so is she.

You may be wondering what is on our list. What do Kim and Nancy value in their friendship in marriage? What are their priorities? What do they focus on? I really debated whether to list them or not because I don't want our list to become your list. You need to make a list that fits your marriage together. But here is our list:

- Always be honest with each other, even when it might mean hurt feelings.
- Trust each other and be trustworthy always.
- Be loyal to each other and never let anyone or anything take that away.
- Listen well.
- Support each other.
- Encourage each other.
- Laugh together.
- Empathize with each other.
- Pray for each other.
- Accept each other's differences.

That's about it. We may add something in the future, but today that fits us well.

## THAT'S A WRAP

This chapter was probably easy for some of you and difficult for others. If you are best friends with your spouse, cherish that and keep doing what you have been doing.

Maybe even take it up a notch. It you are drifting, stop. What have you stopped doing that always worked? Talk about it and commit to get back on track. In other words, stop the drift and start swimming toward each other. If the friendship that started this relationship is gone, don't give up. Don't settle for what you don't want. Do something. If your spouse won't work on it with you now, start anyway. Be a friend. Be the best friend they could ever imagine. If you do, I think there is a good chance that at some point they will respond in a good way. Just don't give up!

## KEYS TO FRIENDSHIP

As we complete this chapter, here are some things I want you to think about:

- List three things you have done in the past for fun. Pick one of them to do again soon!
- Set aside time to share the funny things from your marriage that you have laughed about in the past.
- Together start working on your "best friend in marriage" essentials list.
- If there is something in your life that is harming your friendship, agree to work on that together.

*Going Deeper*

Once you have your "essentials list," pick out one essential that you will both work on and focus on for a predetermined period of time. Then work through your list, taking time to focus on each one. As you do this, encourage each other, and share ideas about what works and what does not. Use this process to connect and deepen your friendship with each other. Next time someone asks you who your "bestie" is, I want you to answer "My husband!" or "My wife!" without even having to think.

# CHAPTER 9

# Daily Touch Points: Talking

I know Russell Westbrook. In case you don't, he plays basketball for the Oklahoma City Thunder. He was the NBA Most Valuable Player in 2017. I can tell you his stats. I can tell you where he lives and all kinds of interesting information about him. I can tell you his wife's name and the name of his first child. I can tell you where he grew up, where he went to school, and when he was drafted by an NBA team. I can tell you all of that and more about Russell Westbrook because I Googled him. I already knew many of the things that Google told me, but I learned a lot that I did not know.

Now back to my first statement. Do I really know Russell Westbrook? No. I know a lot about him, but I don't know him. I've never even been introduced to Russell. His wife, brother, and extended family know Russell. They know what he does each day, what he thinks about, what he worries about, and what he likes and does not like. They know Russell in deep and intimate ways. I don't.

I know Nancy Kimberling. I know everything about her

without ever doing a Google search. Besides, I know so much more than Google knows about her. We met when she was eighteen and have spent as much time as we could together since then. I know what she does each day, what she likes, what she does not like, what she worries about, and much, much more. I know her. Knowing Nancy on a deep, intimate level is a big part of what makes our marriage work. Her knowledge of me is equally intimate. Knowing each other at this level is part of what the Bible is talking about when it says "the two become one." We know each other.

On a scale of one to ten, with ten being the highest, how well do you know your spouse? Now that you have your number, how do you feel about it? Is it where you want it to be? Is it lower or higher? Is it where you expected to be at this point in your marriage? When Nancy and I married, I knew her. We spent two years getting to know each other, and what I knew of her was why I wanted to marry her. Do I know her better today? Absolutely. But that did not just happen. If all I knew about Nancy was what I knew after two years, I would have missed out on so much. Through the years of our marriage, we have had thousands of touch points that have taken our knowledge of each other to new levels. They bonded us closer to each other and they still do.

Most of us can think of at least one couple that just "exists" together in their marriage. They are strangers living in the same house, and most of them are in that situation because they didn't take advantage of the touch point opportunities that were in front of them every day.

In our marriage, we have gone through a few seasons of "existing." Looking back, I hated those times. It was so far away from what I wanted our marriage to be. With God's help, we made it through those seasons and embraced daily touch points again.

Knowing Nancy gives me not only outward joy but also inward joy. Knowing her meets those needs God placed inside of me for her to meet. Do you want that for the two of you? That's what this chapter is all about. No matter what your "knowing" number is today, it can get better by just looking for and taking advantage of the touch points that are right in front of you every single day.

### LIAM AND MADISON

Almost without exception, the couples I talk to say that at one time in their marriage they really knew each other or were at least on the right track to deepening their knowledge of each other. When they quit growing together, something changed. It probably did not happen all at once. One day they were too busy to recognize the touch point opportunities in front of them. Then there were more days without a touch point than there were touch point days. Finally, one or both of them looked up and realized that they were just living together. They had become two roommates. They may or may not have been fighting, but they definitely didn't know each other in the way they used to.

Enter Liam and Madison. We all know that we have

expectations in our marriages. We have talked about not sharing expectations with each other and how detrimental that can be to a marriage. We get in a pattern of being dis-appointed or at times angry with our spouse for not meet-ing the expectations we have of them—whether we have communicated them or not. For Liam and Madison, none of the above fit them at all. Liam came from a good home, as society would define it. His parents had married young and stayed married—something you get bonus points for today. His dad was president of his company and had worked hard to attain that role. His mom stayed at home with the children and was very involved in society and vol-unteer activities. Liam heard the words "you have such a wonderful family" more times than he could count, and he believed every word.

Liam came into marriage wanting to model his parents. No one would have argued that point with him. If we could become invisible and spend a week in Liam's parents' home, what would we see? We would see a husband and a wife who were very nice to each other. They never argued. Each had their own interests, but they had none in com-mon. The house was quiet and peaceful, primarily because there was no talking. Touch points came and went each day as they had for years without anyone grabbing on to them. So Liam came into marriage without one single expectation of knowing Madison any better in the future than he did on their wedding day.

Madison grew up as an only child in a single-parent home. She never met her father. As great as Madison's mom was, there was no modeling of what marriage was supposed to look like for Madison. As she entered marriage, it seemed only right that they model their marriage after Liam's parents' because theirs seemed so perfect. What we have here is a perfect recipe for a long-term marriage between two strangers, and that is exactly what I saw in them when they sat in my office after eight years of marriage. Madison made the appointment and Liam came willingly, but with no idea why they were seeing a counselor. Madison had difficulty expressing why they were there too. She said, "I just think there should be something more to our marriage."

The easy part in counseling them was that they didn't bring any marriage-damaging baggage with them. They never fought and were so nice to each other. My role was to get them to see that they were missing touch points every day that could take their marriage to a level they never knew existed. Madison was all in. Liam was, too, even though he couldn't see how things could get any better than they already were. All I asked them to do the first week was to identify touch point opportunities and write them down. The next time I saw them, Madison had a very long list. Liam's was considerably shorter, but at least he'd made the effort. The next step was to begin taking advantage of those opportunities. Here are some of the touch points they began to take advantage of:

- When they both arrived home in the evenings, they would usually greet each other and then go their separate ways. Now they sat down together and talked about their day.

- When Madison had an errand to run and Liam was home, she invited him to go with her and he did.
- On the ride home from church, they discussed the sermon note questions in the bulletin.
- They were in the habit of not eating dinner together. Each would eat when they were hungry or had time. Now they were intentional about eating together without any other distractions.
- They already prayed together as husband and wife but it was very sporadic. Each night at bedtime they began to share concerns and pray silently together. They also committed to go to bed at the same time.
- Their sex life was erratic and would have long lapses between occurrences. They committed to be much more intentional about it. (Going to bed together was a big step in the right direction.)

The next time I saw them, I could hardly get Liam to stop talking so I could hear from Madison. He loved what was happening in their marriage. He said, "I really think that I am getting to know Madison in ways I never did before." Over the next few months, I saw incredible growth in their marriage. They were finding new touch points every week. They were beginning to know each other in ways that bonded them closer and closer to each other. The days of being strangers living in the same house were over.

What did you identify with in Liam and Madison's story?

Are there touch point opportunities you can identify and begin taking advantage of together? What if you added just one new touch point to your marriage every week for a month? God certainly desires for us to know him at more intimate levels and to grow in our relationship with Him. He desires the same for the two of you in your marriage.

## A "KIND" OF COMMUNICATION

I have a good friend who is an engineer. He can figure things out and design and build amazing machines. At home, he can barely change a lightbulb, much to the frustration of his wife. For me, I love counseling couples, giving them ideas, helping them work through problems, and making their marriages better. At home, my batting average fluctuates. As a counselor, knowing how to do something and helping others do that something is easy for me. Knowing how to make a marriage better and then doing so every day in my marriage is not always easy. This is my dilemma. Home is my refuge. Home is where I let my hair down. Sometimes I can go too far. I don't live alone. I have a wife who loves me, who needs and wants me to be a part of her life. So when I get short with her because I am tired or frustrated or whatever, the results are never good. I get down on myself because I know better. And they are not good for her because I have let her down and often even pushed her away.

For our marriage to get better, something needed to

change, and that something was me. I also knew that this was like anything else in my life that needed to change. I could not do it alone. The only one who could really help me was God. So I began to pray. I asked Him to change my attitude and tone of voice and the words I said. "Help me to be kind," I pleaded. Kind communication. What a simple concept. Kind words. Kind tone of voice. Kind body language. Kind. What happened was a total God deal. It was one of those times that I prayed and He showed up.

This time I opened myself up completely to Him. I had the motivation and the desire. "Change me," I said. There were times that I opened my mouth and could hardly believe the words that came out. Don't get me wrong, I didn't become God's puppet; but then, in a way, maybe I did. Not in a bad way—in an incredibly good way. When I laid down my selfish ways and desires, I opened myself to Him and His ways. My words became kinder, my body language became kinder, and my tone of voice was kinder. Then Nancy's response was amazing. She was kinder too. We both loved what was happening. It changed our interactions. Do I still get off track at times? Sure, but He gets me back on quickly, and I tell Nancy that I am sorry and we move on.

Think about your conversations with your spouse yesterday. How many of them were kind conversations? For the ones that were not, what could you have done to reframe them into kind conversations? What can you learn from this exercise? Remember to start with step one: pray. You can't do it on your own. Believe me, I tried. I don't know why it was so hard for me to be consistent in this way. Actually, I do know. My selfishness was ruling my life. It trumped Nancy and God. How was that working for me? Not well at all. Being kind can have an amazing effect on you, your spouse, and your marriage. It creates lots of touch points. What are you waiting on?

## PILLOW TALK

A movie called *Pillow Talk* was released in 1959, starring two of Hollywood's most popular actors of that era, Rock Hudson and Doris Day. The plot centered on two main characters who shared a common phone line, which apparently was not unusual during that time period. The girl developed a strong dislike for the guy because he was basically hustling a number of women. The common phone line allowed her to hear some of his conversations, which she found very offensive. Though they shared a line, she had never seen this guy. The plot thickens as they meet and he takes on a separate identity and voice. She has no idea that this charming man is actually the same person she loathes. He begins to romance her with long romantic phone conversations in the evening. The pillow talk comes into play as the conversations continue, becoming more intimate as each is in bed, although each in their own apartment. As with most movies there is more to the story and, of course, some plot twists. It is a classic romantic comedy from that time period.

The definition of "pillow talk" that resonates with me most from the *Urban Dictionary* is: "Pillow talk can be any variety of things. It can be before or after being intimate, or without that at all. The point of pillow talk, though, is for two people to enjoy each other's presence through conversation, in a somewhat spontaneous way, but in a way that will let both parties go to bed with clear heads." Pillow talk has always been a part of our marriage. I think it served a variety of purposes as we went through different stages of marriage. Before we had kids, it was just one more way to spend time together. The whole event of being married and getting to have someone of the opposite sex spend the night in your bed every night was awesome. It took us a couple of years for that to become normal. It was one of those early touch points in our marriage, and we really did not understand how much it did for our marriage. Sex was a big part of this, but we also saw the value in pillow talk before and after sex and on the nights that didn't include sex.

The first change in this routine came with our first child. There were late-night feedings, middle-of-the-night feedings, and early morning feedings, and lots of times in the early months when one pillow in our bed was empty. We learned to take advantage of the pillow talk times when they occurred. If it was the middle of the night, early morning, or whenever we were both in bed, we took the time to talk.

Once our kids were a little older, pillow talk returned to bedtime. The difference was that there were a lot of nights that Nancy wanted to talk and I was exhausted. I know she was tired, too, but pillow talk was a priority for her. Knowing that helped motivate me to stay awake to be with her. That and the couple of times I fell asleep in the middle of her sharing something and received a wake-up call in the form of a thrown pillow. In those situations, I can be a quick learner. Once our kids were off to college, we got back into our pre-kids mode. Today we have a lot of touch points in our day but we both agree that pillow talk is probably our favorite. There are so many good things that come out of it in addition to sex.

So how is your pillow talk? Is it more than sex? Go back to the definition. Is it a time for the two of you "to enjoy each other's presence through conversation?" Does it let you both go to sleep "with clear heads"? Is it a touch point that you are taking advantage of?

DIGGING FURTHER

There are a number of different ways we communicate. For the most part, I think women get this concept better than men. Sorry, guys. It seems that we are pretty satisfied with regular everyday conversations that don't go deep. We can talk about sports, something we saw in the news, a vacation, and our kids' activities without blinking an eye. That seems to fill our need for daily conversation most of the time. The problem with all of this is that you are married to a woman. She is probably fine with the above *but* she wants more. She wants to know what you think about the news and how you feel about things. She wants to know

your ideas and opinions. These are things that come easy
for her and that are hard for most of us men. This is where
many couples get in a standoff. She wants more. He is satisfied with less. Usually a woman pursues and tries to let
him know this is important to her, but if he continues not to
respond, she may eventually give up. That's not good. Not
good at all. She had a need that she wanted her husband to
meet and he didn't. Now what does she do?

This is what I know. Most guys never had deeper conversations modeled. Most guys are scared to death of being
vulnerable. Most guys don't want to go deep, and we can
do all kinds of unhealthy things to keep from going there.
Here is my counsel: First, pray for God to help you. Second,
agree to try. Just a commitment to do that at some level will
be encouraging to your wife. Third, start slow. Instead of
just sharing information with her, also share what you think
about it or any ideas you had from that information. (You
just made a huge step forward and I'm guessing you are
still breathing.) The fourth step is a little tricky, but you can
take it slow as long as you don't get stuck. You have to keep
moving forward. This is where you share what you feel, and
this doesn't mean screaming because you are angry. Think
about it this way. You are not sharing your feelings with the
world; you are sharing them with the person who chose to
live her life with you. The person who longs for a deeper
relationship with you. God equipped her to come alongside
you in this. Set your fear aside and go for it.

Here is a hypothetical situation. At work today, Bob was
fired. It came out of the blue. He wasn't your best friend, but

Bob is a good guy and you enjoyed talking with him. Usually, when you get home, you would say something like, "Hey, Bob got fired today. I hate that. He's a good guy." What if you just take it a step further by saying something like, "Sometimes I think my company is unfair. I don't like that about them," or you could go deeper and say, "Deep down it scares me that the same thing could happen to me." Sure, that is a little risky, but I promise you that your wife (after she comes to) will be right there with you and encouraging you. The first time is the hardest, but this is what I think will happen: you will feel better and you will experience the freedom that comes with vulnerability. One other thing: I'm not saying that you have to do this every day, but get comfortable with it so the days you need to go there, you can.

Now to the ladies. When he takes that risk, your role is to affirm him and encourage him. If it goes pretty well the first time, then there is a good chance it will happen again and again.

Guys, what is your biggest fear in doing this? How about sharing that with your wife? Finally, God will equip you in this. He wants you to trust Him. Going deeper hits touch points that otherwise would go untouched. Don't miss these opportunities.

## TALKING TIME

If we define touch points as talking time together as a couple, how much time do we need each day? I'm not going to tell you, but I am going to give you some questions to consider as you think through it. Be really honest with each other: How much time are you spending together each day, on average? This is actual talking time not just being in the same vicinity at home. Now, whatever number you came up with, is it enough? Is the time you spend talking each day giving you enough touch points to meet your needs and grow your marriage? My guess is that most of you are saying no. That's why I did not give you an answer. It varies.

If you are doing a pretty good job with talk time, you may decide to increase it a little each day until you feel it is meeting your needs, or you may look for additional opportunities to have touch points. If your number of minutes was zero or just a few, you are probably going to want to be very proactive in building these times into your married life. People used to ask me whether quality of time or quantity of time was more important. My answer was always both. However much time you have, make it the best quality possible. As you work on the quality of your time together, add as much quantity as you can. If you make this a checklist for so many minutes each day, you are missing the point and probably won't get what you want and need out of it.

Sit down with each other and brainstorm ideas of possible touch points in your day. When do you have opportunities? What are some opportunities that you are not taking advantage of? Be creative. I counseled a couple who added showering together in the morning before the kids got up as a touch point. Another couple started looking through Facebook together and talking about what was going on in their Facebook worlds. Cooking together, cleaning together, doing projects together, running errands together, and exercising together all are opportunities to have talk time. It just takes focus. You can do all of the above in silence or you can take advantage of them and add some touch points to your day. From your brainstorm list, add one thing. My hope is that as you are intentional about this, you will see the value in the times you are adding and will look for more touch point opportunities.

## KEYS TO DAILY TOUCH POINTS

As we complete this chapter, here are some things I want you to think about:

- What are your current touch point opportunities as a couple? What do you need to do to take advantage of them each day?
- What is one new touch point you will add to your marriage?
- What does "kind communication" mean to you in your marriage? Is this an area for the two of you to work on together?
- What is one talk time that you will add to your marriage?

*Going Deeper*

Every touch point that you create in your marriage is an opportunity for the two of you to go deeper. Touch points create talk time. There is so much value in simply focusing on each other when you have a touch point. Touch points alone will grow your marriage. You will be intentional. You will focus on enjoying being together. You will be creative in finding these times. Just don't miss the chance to go to deeper levels of talking. If you think something, say it. If you feel something, express it. If you have an opinion about something, share it. Digging deeper will build your marriage and draw you even closer to each other.

# CHAPTER 10

# Sex: How Often?

Let's begin this chapter with a series of questions: How often do married couples have sex? What is normal? If you seldom have sex, does this affect your marriage in a negative way? How does the quality versus quantity thing work in regard to sex? Can you have too much sex? How often do you have sex?

Sex has been a part of marriage since Adam looked at a naked and unashamed Eve and said, "Wow!" Okay, that is not exactly in the Bible, but I cannot imagine him saying anything else! How often did Adam and Eve have sex? I have no idea, but from creation to Genesis 3 when they disobeyed God and were clothed, there was a lot of nakedness. Let's get back to the questions. How often do married couples have sex? There have been a number of studies on this, and the consensus seems to land at a little over one time a week. For some couples it is more often than this; for others it is less. How often you and your spouse have sex is probably not something you want to compare with other couples. Defining what is normal can be difficult.

There is so much to be considered. Marriages are different, lives are different, and schedules are different. What do you consider normal for you as a couple? If you have sex once a week, twice a month, or once a month, does that work for you both? Most couples who fight over sex seem to fight over frequency. And most of those couples don't talk about it until one of them wants to have sex, which is usually not the optimal time. I don't think I have ever talked about sex with a couple who both had the exact same sex drive. One usually wants to have sex more often than the other. Totally normal.

Frequency is not the issue—though most couples miss this point. The issue is *how* you together handle the frequency issue. Do you talk about it? Do you empathize with each other? Do you compromise? When we fight over frequency, our focus shifts and we are no longer embracing the gift of sex in marriage as God intended. It is important to define together what is your normal at this stage of your marriage. It's not meant to be a rigid rule, and it will get you to discuss sex, which is good. Let's say you decide that twice a week works for both of you.

Some couples find they need to schedule it. Most of us cringe at this thought because sex is supposed to be spontaneous. I agree that spontaneous sex is great, but nowhere is it written that sex must be that way. Scheduling helps when schedules are busy or you have kids in the house. One couple I know found that scheduling sex on Sunday afternoons during the kids' nap time worked well for them. It could be a weeknight when the kids go to bed early so you can have alone time together. My point is don't be afraid of scheduling if it helps with frequency. One wife shared with me that scheduling actually helped her get her mind focused on having sex with her husband. This was a big plus for her. Even if we don't put it on the calendar (which can be fun and get some interesting messaging going on in the day), most of us know when there are consistent windows of opportunity for sex in our marriage on any given week. Your normal may not be twice a week. It may be more, less, or far less. The key here is: Does it work for both of you? If it does, I would say that's your normal. Embrace it!

Before we move on, let's talk for a minute about this whole quantity versus quality thing. We have defined the quantity by deciding on your normal. Now the quality. How do you define quality sex? Be careful here that you don't create a box that you cannot get out of. For my wife and me, quality means that we both enjoy the experience. Does it mean that we both have an orgasm every time? No. If we define successful sex only by reaching orgasm, I think we run the risk of missing out on some great experiences. Usually if one doesn't have an orgasm, it's the woman. At least, that's what women tell me. But even if they don't have an orgasm, they enjoy the experience: it feels good; they love the closeness; they love the attention and intimacy. As guys, we can feel that we failed if our wife does not climax. So listen up: That is not the gauge. Don't miss the experience because you bought into that idea.

Quality does not mean that every time you have sex there has to be candlelight, special music, or hours of foreplay. A quickie in the morning can offer just as much quality as a two-hour session in the evening. They are different but equally valuable. Remember the standard here is that you both enjoy the experience. For the men, there is usually no bad sex. A man's mind can go to sex in a split second or less, but a woman usually needs a little time to focus and warm up to the idea. I know that when I give Nancy time, we both enjoy the experience even more.

US

I could give you a lot of examples of couples' struggles with sex and how they worked through those, but there is only one couple's story that I know firsthand from day one until today. So here is our story.

Let's get the twenty-two-year-old new husband honeymoon experience out of the way first. That story began two years earlier when I met Nancy on a blind date. She was nothing like what I expected. When I saw her, she literally took my breath away and I stammered like I had never learned to speak. For two years I dreamed of being married to her and having sex all the time. Sorry, that's just the way it was. Which brings us to our honeymoon. I thought we needed a quota of three times a day. It made total sense to me. Did I share that with Nancy? No. So by day three I'm sure she wondered what she had married. There was some good that came out of my quota system, though, because by the end of the honeymoon we had our first sex talk. She felt I was being too rigid, not letting our sex life develop and be spontaneous. She was right. In the first years of our marriage, frequency was not a problem. Spontaneity worked well for us. We never turned each other down. We were never too tired for sex. It was an important part of our marriage and was really good for both of us. Our friendship drew us together, and we never wanted to lose that with each other. Sex bonded us in the same way.

Our first hurdle was one many couples face: babies. After five years of marriage we were ready for our family to grow. We loved having a baby in our lives and embraced the changes that came with it, but sex became a challenge. I'd ask Nancy at bedtime if she wanted to have sex. She'd say yes and then she'd fall asleep before I could get my clothes off. Both of us, but especially Nancy, experienced fatigue on a whole new level. The energy that had always been there for sex was now often difficult to find. I was frustrated, and she hated that I was frustrated. The key for me was to realize that we were simply in a different season, and it would not last forever.

Acceptance was huge for me. Acceptance made our new-found life together much easier to deal with and took the pressure off of Nancy. Those seasons come into all of our sex lives. Accepting and adjusting makes the difference. Our frequency changed but once I accepted it, our quality didn't suffer. The reality of one and then two extra little people in our house was something we both cherished, but it was a time of challenges in our sex life. We had to talk more, plan more, and embrace the changes. There were some changes that really helped. We began to lock our bedroom door. We knew there were opportunities that we needed to take advantage of. If a grandparent stopped by to take the kids for ice cream, we had an opportunity. If both kids had a playdate with friends at their house, we had an opportunity. Don't jump to conclusions though—we didn't have sex every time the kids were gone! Sometimes we took a nap or watched a movie or worked in the yard.

Did we have problems with our sex life? Yes. Looking back, most of them were caused by my constant physical attraction to Nancy. For us both to enjoy the sexual experience consistently, I needed to be aware of and meet her needs. Nancy likes to cuddle. But when I was that close to her, not initiating sex seemed like a hurdle I could not get over. Nancy needed nonsexual touching times. She needed times of conversation when we were alone. Instead of just enduring these times of nonsexual touching and conversation, doing them to "check off a box," I actually learned to enjoy them. Over time it even enhanced our sexual relationship. We felt more deeply connected to each other.

Many of you reading this will be in the child-raising season of your marriage, or getting ready for that season. Know that you will have to make adjustments to keep your sexual relationship a priority, but it is worth it! Sex bonds us together in very special ways: physical, emotional, mental, and spiritual. The Hebrews had an amazing word for this, "dod," meaning "a mingling of souls." It is a connection at our deepest core, but like anything else in life that is worthwhile, you have to be intentional to build, maintain, and grow it.

Because we did a pretty good job of being intentional, we've come into the empty-nest season of life ready to enjoy each other more fully. We have more time for each other. Do we miss the times with our kids, helping with homework and going to events and games? Of course. But we are also able to see all God has for us in this new era. We have flexibility and the ability to do things we chose not to do in the past. By taking advantage of these opportunities to be together and grow together, guess what happened? Our sex life has gotten even better. It was like we took a big step forward in the whole "two become one" deal. The house is ours. Sex can be more spontaneous now.

Nancy and I are very open about our sexual relationship, the successes and failures. We see sex in marriage as a great gift from God and want every couple to experience it in its fullness. Don't settle for less. We strive for a "ten" in every area of our marriage, including our sex life. We don't always get there, but we want to keep the standard high.

How do you rate your sex life in your marriage today? What would it take to get it to a nine or ten? The first step is to spend time talking about it with your spouse. If you feel you cannot do that without help, go to a Christian counselor or someone you trust in this area. Sex is not the easiest subject to discuss, but things will not improve on their own. What will the two of you commit to do?

## PROBLEMS, PROBLEMS

Let's look at four problem areas that affect sex in marriage:

1.  Are you both getting your sexual needs met?
2.  Is low libido an issue for either one of you?

3.  Do you prioritize your sex life?
4.  Do you feel relaxed and comfortable in your own sexuality?

**Are you both getting your sexual needs met?**

When you think about sexual needs being met, what comes to your mind? How would your spouse answer that question? This question is influenced by our gender. Most studies agree that sex is a physical need for men. Not to get into a discussion here, but a man's desire for sex is influenced not only by his circumstances or the environment around him but also by testosterone levels and other biological factors. When a man has sex, that need is satisfied but will build again. Women, on the other hand, are different. Hormones fluctuate, affecting their sex drive. Most men can be stimulated easily most of the time. I can look at Nancy and think about having sex with her when that idea is nowhere on her radar. That truth for men probably comes as no surprise. How we handle these differences and needs is important and can make or break sex in your marriage.

Audrey and Andrew were at odds. The presenting problem when they came to see me was bad communication. About halfway through their first session, talk turned to the topic of sex. Sex was a problem. Audrey thought Andrew wanted sex all the time, and Andrew thought Audrey never wanted sex. It wasn't always that way for them though. They met when both of them were in their mid-twenties. Both had dated other people off and on in the past, and both had had a long-term relationship that did involve sex and did not work out. Both felt that sex had changed the previous relationships, and didn't want the same result again. After a year of dating, Andrew proposed and Audrey excitedly said yes. Sex had become a part of their relationship while dating, but only a handful of times. They never fought about sex but were not ready for it to become center stage in their relationship. There would be plenty of time for that in marriage. I like their story because it is one that many couples deal with. Sex was great on the honeymoon, good in marriage, and crashed after year three. When sex crashes in a marriage, there can be a number of reasons: pregnancies, job demands, busy schedules, and fatigue can all play a part.

For Audrey and Andrew, the issue was their jobs. Both were doing well in their respective companies, but doing well meant more responsibility, longer hours, and more traveling. They settled into a pattern that was killing them. With both traveling during the week, Friday night was set aside for them to be alone. Great idea. The problem was that they approached Friday with different agendas. Audrey wanted to hang out, talk, share about her week, and hear about Andrew's. Andrew wanted sex, and that trumped talking, hanging out, or anything else. He said, "If we could just have sex, then I could do the other things she wants me to do." She said, "If he would just hang out and talk with me, sex would eventually happen." Sound familiar at all? For Audrey and Andrew, this became their weekly pattern. Both were frustrated and angry, and no one was budging. If you were their counselor, what would you tell them? Take some time together and see if you can come up with a solution that would help Andrew and Audrey solve their problem. I'll share my input later.

### Is low libido an issue for either one of you?

Low libido is simply the loss of sexual desire. Most of us will experience this at some time in our marriage. Let's make a list of possible causes: severe illness, depression, some antidepressants or other medications, stress, poor body image, poor self-image, marriage issues, and sexual performance anxieties. You may add other causes, but this gives us a basis for our discussion. When I talk to a couple about low libido, I want to check out the common problems first. Is there depression? Have they talked to their doctor about their libido problem? Have they had blood work done to confirm or rule out causes? What stresses are they under? What medications are they on? Is lower libido a side effect? Then we can begin to look at marriage issues or personal issues that may be affecting their sex drive. Whatever the problem, there is hope. Low libido is not usually something a couple has to live with the rest of their marriage. It is a combination of a good doctor, a good Christian counselor, and the couple themselves all working together to get to the bottom of the problem and to chart a plan of healing.

Samuel and Lily had not had sex in over one year when I saw them. There was a time in their marriage that both agreed the sex was good. It was never once a week, but when they had sex they both were satisfied. The problem began when Samuel slid into depression. Like most men, Samuel did not immediately seek help. He had never been depressed in his life. He was not even sure what depression was all about, but he knew he was tired, irritable, and not interested in anything—especially sex. Lily's mind went to a lot of places that were unhealthy for her. "What's wrong with him?" "Why is he not interested in me?" "Is he having an affair?" The longer they went without having sex, the harder it was to get it going again. They did try once about four months into the drought but Samuel could not get an erection. He was humiliated, and afraid the same thing would happen again. Samuel had never had a problem with erections in the past, and Lily began to be very self-conscious about her body. Finally, sex was taken off the table. They were not fighting anymore but both wanted things to get back to their sexual "normal." It's your turn again. As their counselor, what would you advise them to do? What would be their next step? I'll give you my perspective later.

### Do you prioritize your sex life?

When I ask a couple if their sex life is important to them, I have never heard a couple answer no. But when I then ask them how they prioritize it, I usually hear nothing in response. For most couples, life, kids, and busyness become part of the daily routine, and sex gets pushed down the list. It's not like they are against sex or don't like sex;

they just aren't taking any steps toward making it a real priority.

Anthony and Savannah were one of those couples. Verbally, they agreed that sex was a priority. Their small group at church had done a study on sex, and Anthony and Savannah quickly agreed that sex in their marriage was a priority of "ten." That's where the small group study ended. No one talked about action steps or what worked for them as a couple. Everyone went home, knowing the next week they would start a new study on parenting.

The following day during her quiet time, Savannah pulled out her calendar. She liked a paper calendar where she could see the entire month at a glance. Savannah was very organized—probably a little over the top. Savannah, Anthony, and each of their three kids had a different color code on her calendar. It was easy for her to see every day what each person had to do, and she could plan her day accordingly. For that month there were two entries in blue for Anthony. Those were their date nights. As she flipped back to the month prior, both date nights were scratched out and replaced with a different color entry. She knew there was a good chance the same thing would happen this month. If she was honest with herself, even when they had a date night it seldom ended with sex. Their new normal was one or two times a month at best, and for them that was not good. Plus she knew they had both lied to their small group. It was hard to be honest with others about their sex life. Now you have a good overview of Anthony and Savannah.

If you were their counselor, what would you tell them to do? I'll give you my perspective in a bit.

### Do you feel relaxed and comfortable in your own sexuality?

How we see ourselves sexually plays a big part in our sex lives in marriage. In our culture, I think women struggle in this area more than men do. A woman cannot go anywhere without seeing something that depicts the "perfect look" or the "perfect body." Whether it is the magazine rack at the grocery store checkout, the latest movie, or a billboard you pass every day on the freeway, the temptation to compare yourself to someone else is everywhere. I know it's not fair. Plus, most photos are airbrushed. Hollywood can transform anyone into perfection. It just takes a few hours of preparation, makeup, and a little extra help here and there. The problem is that many ladies have bought into this mess hook, line, and sinker. The answer is simple: stop. Stop comparing. Stop believing that you have to look a certain way to be attractive to your husband. Start believing him when he tells you that you are beautiful and sexy and that he wants only you. Remember he chose you and you chose him. Remember what God says about you. "I praise you, for I am fearfully and wonderfully made" (Ps. 139:14 ESV). You are perfect in God's eyes. He does not make mistakes. He sees who you are inside and the beauty of your heart. I have counseled so many women who buy into unrealistic beauty as culture defines it. They struggle to see themselves through God's eyes and to embrace the love their spouses give them. Until you do, you are missing out on so much. Listen to God. Listen to your husband. Rejoice in who you are!

I know some guys struggle in this area too. If that is you, everything I applied to your wife applies to you. See yourself through God's eyes and believe her when she says, "You're hot!"

Addison looked in the mirror and never liked what she saw. Luke wasn't the first guy to tell her she was beautiful, but she knew they all had ulterior motives. A guy would say anything to get a girl in bed. She fell for that once but never again. The next day at school the guy acted as though she didn't exist. That was a long time ago, though, and Luke was different in so many ways. He said some of the same things the other guys said, but he never pushed past that. He never tried anything sexual, and they dated for over two years. When he asked her to marry him, she knew she would be a fool to say no. She did think she had figured out Luke's plan. She thought he would tell her she was beautiful until she said yes and married him. Then he could have sex with her and didn't have to lie about her beauty anymore. That's what she thought, but Addison decided she didn't care what his plan might be. She loved him deeply and wanted to believe he felt the same about her. In marriage, to her shock, nothing changed. He told her daily that he loved her and that she was beautiful. Yes they had sex, but it was beautiful too. It took a few years before Addison truly believed that the words Luke said were true. Looking in the mirror today is different for her. She finally sees herself through God's and Luke's eyes. What a difference it has made.

The body image issue can affect how comfortable and relaxed we are when having sex with our spouse. If you are thinking about what he or she is thinking, you are going to miss out on a lot of the enjoyment that comes with sex. I have counseled couples who have never had sex with the lights on or seen each other naked in the light. Go back to Adam and Eve. Remember how they were described: "Naked and unashamed." To me that means first they had absolutely no clothes on and they were not hiding from each other. They were walking around nude day or night. Now for the "unashamed" part. I think that means that they were very comfortable with each other and their naked bodies. They were completely vulnerable and completely trusted each other. That was God's plan. Still is. I believe Jesus redeemed everything for us so that, as Christians, we could have what Adam and Eve had. We just have to battle through cultural messages and other baggage to get there.

If you are feeling uncomfortable now, don't worry. I'm not telling you to get naked and run around the house together all day, but if you want to, go for it. What I am saying is: Don't sell yourself short. If you are having sex only in the dark under the sheets, take a step toward naked and unashamed. Maybe you turn a table lamp on or kick the covers off and let the moonlight come through the window. Begin to get comfortable with who you are and who your spouse is sexually. Some people may need counseling if they suffered abuse or other trauma. Take the time to do that. Usually one spouse is more comfortable than the other with the whole naked and unashamed scenario. Your role is to gently encourage your spouse. Don't push. It may take time. Praise them for the smallest step forward. Be a part of counseling if they ask you to. Know that you are not alone in this. I cannot think of any other gift from God that has been perverted like sex in marriage, but this is not a battle that you will let the enemy win. Together you can receive the gift in all its goodness just as God designed.

## MY TURN

You have had the opportunity to play counselor. I'm going to give you my perspective on the three couples you read about. This is not a right-or-wrong issue. If your answer is different from mine, you may have discovered something I overlooked. The idea was to get you thinking proactively about how to solve problems in marriage.

### A Solution for Audrey and Andrew

You probably guessed that Audrey and Andrew were both very strong-willed people. They needed a point of compromise. I suggested they begin with this: Next Friday when they both were home, they would sit down together and hang out and talk for at least an hour. During that time they were to listen well and both engage in the talk. Then later that evening, sex was at the top of the agenda for both. The following Friday they were to reverse the order. Sex first, hang out second. I was not sure how they would take it, but they really liked it. Was that the best long-term solution for them? Maybe and maybe not, but at that time it was a win-win for them, and that was what they needed.

### A Solution for Samuel and Lily

Samuel and Lily let a problem that could really have some good solutions turn into a monster in their marriage by not getting help sooner. Samuel was depressed. It affected his libido and thus his erections. Lily had so many unhealthy thoughts that she was in danger of slipping into depression too. I referred Samuel to a doctor to help treat his depression. The doctor was sensitive to the erection issue as he put Samuel on medication. Antidepressant medication takes a while to work. I encouraged them to wait until Samuel felt the effects of the medication before trying sex. During that time, I met with both of them together to talk through the thoughts and assumptions they made during their sexless year. Samuel also met with me to work on the causes of his depression, which allowed the medication to be that much more effective. Over the next couple of months, their sex life returned to their normal. They were very content with this. Samuel stayed on the antidepressant for a little over a year, and then his doctor had him gradually wean himself off. The depression didn't return.

### A Solution for Anthony and Savannah

For Anthony and Savannah, the evidence of the issue was Savannah's calendar. The family schedule was out of control, and the only entries that were flexible involved their marriage. The emotions that came with the chaos began with the calendar. I was not going to ask them to change everything at once but to make a plan to implement over the next few months. They agreed that the kids were in way too many activities. I asked them to have a family meeting to explain to the kids what they were doing and why, and to get the kids' input on activities. The response from their kids was amazing. All three liked the idea and said, "Now we can have time to play with the kids in the neighborhood" and "Does this mean I can build with my Legos more?" The teenager said, "I can take a nap after school." It took a while, but by the next school semester there were a lot less colored places on the calendar for the kids and more places for Anthony and Savannah.

### KEYS TO BETTER SEX

As we complete this chapter, here are some things I want you to think about:

- What have you decided together is your "normal" for sex in your marriage? What are you doing to make that "normal" happen?
- Identify one hurdle that you need to work on together to improve your sex life.
- Make a list together of your sexual needs. Put his needs on one side of the list and her needs on the other. Now pick one need from each other's list to focus on.

- Make one decision together that prioritizes your sex life in marriage.

---

*Going Deeper*

If you read this chapter and nothing changes, what happens? Unless your sex life is a consistent "ten" day in and day out, something needs to happen. Maybe it's frequency. Your normal may need an upgrade. We have found that changing routines can add a spark to your sex life. Just make sure you are both comfortable with the changes.

Looking at sex from God's perspective is completely foreign to many people. When we think about sex, we imagine God in this box with the word "prude" marked all over it. Really? God created sex. He made our bodies the way they do to perfectly fit together. If you have not read *Song of Solomon* together, I encourage you to do so. It is a great picture of a husband and a wife romancing each other and completely enjoying each other's bodies. It can change your perspective on how God views sex.

Finally, if your sex life needs help, get it. There is nothing to be ashamed of. Every couple needs help with their sex life at some time in their marriage. The difference is in those who get help and those who do not. Don't be one of the "do nots."

---

# CHAPTER 11

# Flirting and All That Stuff: Intimacy

## FLIRTING

Before marriage, most of us knew how to flirt. It was part of the process. Flirting could cause a number of things to happen for us and the person who was the object of our flirtation. For me, flirting was affirmed when I received a response from the person I was flirting with. I flirted for the first time in second grade. The beginning of that school year brought a new girl to my class. She had blond hair, pigtails, and a killer smile. I was smitten. I had no idea what was going on with me, but I wanted desperately for her to notice me. At recess, we played a lot of different games, but tag was a regular. There she was at the first recess of her first day in her new school standing alone on the playground. This was my chance. I ran over to her and said, "Do you want to play tag?" She said, "Sure." I tagged her, ran off, looked over my shoulder, and was ecstatic that she was running after me.

Flirting was easy. The tactics of flirting changed over the years as we outgrew playing tag. By sixth grade, flirting took the form of smiling at a girl or letting her catch you staring at her. For me, middle school brought new challenges in flirting. The girls were changing. Actually, it wasn't their physical changes that threw me. The attraction to girls was taking a turn that I did not expect. They had new ways to flirt and I didn't know what to do with them. I took a flirting sabbatical so I could regroup.

Nancy came into my life midway through her freshman year at Texas Christian University. I thought I had my flirting game back in good order, but she threw me for a loop at first. I was so attracted to her but my flirting made me look really silly. It was like I was asking her to play tag with me. Fortunately for both of us, I recovered and was back on my game pretty quickly. Flirting was a huge part of our dating relationship. I loved the looks she would give me across a room and how she would let me get lost in her eyes and not turn away. We "studied" together in the school library and played footsie for hours. There was a spark between us, and we were getting really good at keeping it going. The ultimate flirt was the look she gave me on our wedding day as she came down the aisle, which was right before her dad stepped on her wedding veil, jerking her head back. The next look I received from her was a look of *help me!*

Our flirting continued through the honeymoon, our newlywed stage, and on into marriage. We were really good at flirting as a couple and we loved it. The stakes were raised in marriage—there was a new payoff, as sex was now an option. Don't get me wrong, every flirtation didn't (and doesn't) end in sex, but that possibility put a new twist on flirting for us. Flirting away from home today can be a look, a touch, a comment, or almost anything that fires the spark in each of us. At home, it's all of the above plus a sexual component. The essence of flirting is really not that much different from second-grade tag on the playground. It's getting the other person's attention, igniting the spark, and keeping them engaged. It's part of the pursuit.

Do you flirt with each other? If you do, keep it up. If you have let that part of your relationship die out, why not rekindle the fire? My dad's parents were married over fifty years, and I remember them flirting as long as my granddad was alive. He always had this twinkle in his eye and it shone brighter around my grandma. There were the looks and the pats on her rear; he was very affectionate with her. She, on the other hand, was outwardly reserved and I never saw her initiate flirting, but it was the way she received and responded to his flirts that kept the fire lit in their marriage.

I share their story because I think flirting should never stop. It adds to a marriage in a very special way. Sometimes our flirting is a simple word that takes us both back to a special time or event that could be romantic, humorous, or both. It's a connection point that most of the time only the two of us get. If you are thinking, *We have let this die and it's something we need to build back into our marriage*, here are some ideas to get you going:

- How did the two of you flirt when you were dating? What worked? Revisiting some of your flirting from the past is a great place to start.
- Think of some past times that connected you in special ways and revisit them together. Maybe you develop a code word for each to bring back the connection memory in the future.
- Brainstorm together new ways to flirt that fit the two of you today. Then try them out!

## NST

Nonsexual touching has to be a part of your marriage. I know that is a *strong* statement but I feel *strongly* about it. It is another connection point, and I don't want any of us to miss out on the opportunities. Physical touch has always been important to me. My family was a hug-a-lot family and I know it played a big part in how I felt about physical touch.

Sixth grade brought a new ritual to my life in the winter months. Every Saturday, twenty or thirty of us would show up at the local movie house to spend most of the afternoon. This was one of those neighborhood theaters that doesn't exist anymore. They would play two movies back-to-back on Saturday afternoons and there we were, sitting one row in front of the other. It didn't really matter where you sat unless you really liked someone. When that was the case, the entire group worked together so the couple could sit side by side.

On this particular Saturday, I desperately wanted to sit by a certain girl but was afraid to let anyone know my feelings. What I did not know was that she felt the same way about me and was very vocal to her best friends that she wanted to sit by me. As we all filed into the theater, I could not believe that as we sat down, she was right next to me. I would never again doubt that there was a God! In the previous weeks, I observed many of the other guys sitting by a girl they liked. Almost all of them eventually put their arm around the girl. I was not sure if that had to happen, but I was not about to blow this chance.

First, I must have stretched at least ten times to get my arm in the air so it could come down around her, but always chickened out on the downswing. Finally, the first movie was about to end. I made up my mind that when the second movie started, I was making my move, and I did. Success. My arm was now fully around her shoulders. It was awesome until I realized that my arm was falling asleep. Now I had no idea what to do. If I moved my arm, I might never get it in position again, but it was going numb fast. I made the decision to leave it where it was and figure the rest out later. Later came as the second movie ended. She stood up and my arm fell limp. I tried to act like nothing was wrong by using the dead hand to pick up the cup with the rest of my soft drink in it. It was a really clumsy move at best and the cup, ice, and what was left of the drink hit the ground, splashing both of us. My first foray into nonsexual touching crashed and burned.

Often when I speak at a conference and begin to talk

about nonsexual touching, I feel I am losing half my audience—the guys. There are those guys who really never had a use for nonsexual touching in dating or in marriage. Their premise was that it took too much time and delayed the kind of touching they were most interested in. For the other guys, who knew nonsexual touching was the best way to honor a girl while dating, they felt they had paid their dues. Nonsexual touching was the touching you did before marriage. Now that they were married, they had no use for it. Then there was this small group of guys that got it. Nonsexual touching has a place before and in marriage.

For those of us who need a visual, let's define nonsexual touching. It's touching the nonsexual parts. That means breasts and vaginal area are out. You can add some others too. Before marriage, almost any touch I gave Nancy, besides holding her hands, hugging her, and putting my arm around her, was sexual for me. If she asked me to rub her back, it was sexual for me. Playing footsie was not, but rubbing her leg was. So it's probably something other than the obvious that the two of you need to define together. Then, once you are on the same playing field, the next step is cultivating the art of nonsexual touching. You are probably asking, "Why?" or, "Can we skip to chapter 12?" Maybe our story can help.

I don't have to explain how attracted I was to Nancy and how I dreamed of our sexual relationship in marriage. I loved holding her hand, hugging and kissing her, and putting my arm around her—before we were married and after. Here was the difference. I knew that, before marriage, that was it. We were stopping at hand-holding or whatever. Once we were married, in my mind all the barriers were lifted. It was a simple A leads to B, B leads to C, and so on. This worked fine for us for a pretty long time—or at least for me. Then I started to notice that when we were alone, she was not as receptive to the nonsexual touching as before. She would let me hold her hand but then would let it go after a few minutes. The same was true of kissing. She would end the kiss before it got too intense. As a guy, I started analyzing myself first. Deodorant? Check. Cologne she likes? Check. Teeth brushed and mouthwash used? Check. What in the world could be wrong? I then noticed it was carrying over to the bed. The place where she used to lie snuggling close to me was now an empty sheet as she moved away to her side of the bed. Finally, it came out. Nancy very nicely told me, "It seems that every time we touch non-sexually when we are alone, it leads to sex. Before we were married, I really liked holding your hand and hugging you and all the other things. It's not that I don't want sex. I just want to enjoy the other physical aspects too."

It took a little while for that to sink in, and I'm not sure I totally got it. But I knew that if things were going to improve, I had to accept what she was saying. We were in a cycle that I needed to break. She had to trust me again in this area. This was my proposal to her: "I'll make you a deal. I won't let hugs or cuddling or any of those other things turn to sex unless you initiate it." I got one of those looks from her that says, *Are you crazy? Do you think you can really do that?* I said, "Test me." Honestly, a few minutes later I thought that was the stupidest agreement I had ever made. It turned out that it was one of the best. Two things happened. First, I really began to enjoy nonsexual touching again. Second, she began to trust me again. She scooted closer to me in bed and held those kisses longer when we were alone.

What I really want you to gain from this is to value nonsexual touching. It connects you to your spouse and it feels good. Is it as good as sex? No. But it is important. It shows our wives that we value them and the things that are important to them. That alone makes a difference. One other note: after we went through that adjustment in our marriage, our sex life improved big-time.

## ATTRACTION

When you think of attraction, you probably think of the external. For most of us, there was something about our spouse that attracted us the first time we saw them. Since we did not yet know them, it was probably something in the way they looked. Then, as we got to know them, there were other things that attracted us to them. Maybe it was their personality, sense of humor, compassion, or empathy. If we were dependent on physical attraction alone, that would be difficult, because over time our looks change. That's not a bad thing, just a reality of life.

Here is my take on attraction. There are two parts to

this: the outward, physical component and the internal component of our spouse. Over time both will change.

First, the external. As we grow older, our outside appearance changes. I think a person is attractive at every stage of life. We get hung up on the fact that our culture says one particular stage is better than the others. That is not from God. I think Nancy is as beautiful, if not more beautiful, today than the day I first met her. She has a hard time believing that, but I tell her every day. Does she look exactly the same as she did at eighteen? No, but age does not define beauty.

Part of the beauty I see in Nancy comes from the way I see her care for herself. She eats healthy and exercises on a regular basis, for herself, yes, but also for both of us. Our bodies are God's temple and He wants us to care well for this temple. We guys have a responsibility to do the same. I have seen married couples in their nineties who probably barely resemble their wedding pictures from seventy years earlier still gazing at each other with adoring eyes. They are beautiful to each other. If we are given that many years together, I want the same thing for Nancy and me. How about you?

The second part is the internal. My experience tells me this is the important part of attraction. This is where change can make or break a marriage. Let me introduce you to Nora and Wyatt. I didn't know them until they were older and had been married thirty-some years. Wyatt met Nora when she was in her early twenties. She caught his eye at a singles' party hosted by her church. Wyatt was invited by a friend. Nora's long brown hair, dark brown eyes, and dimples all drew him to her. Nora noticed Wyatt because he was tall and handsome and seemed to smile all the time. They met and then dated for almost two years before marriage. Nora was compassionate and cared for others in a way that Wyatt had never experienced. It wasn't just the special way she made him feel but the way she made everyone who knew her feel. His family loved her and so did his friends. He could not have been happier. Wyatt was smart and stable. Nora saw in him a man who could love deeply, who took the role of leadership seriously. She was very secure in the love they had for each other.

Over the next few years, they had a fairly normal life. There were bumps but they always regrouped well and moved on. They had a boy first and two years later, a girl, and both agreed that was it. Nora brought a couple of their wedding pictures to one of their early counseling sessions. It was obvious that externally they both had taken good care of themselves. The changes in them were on the inside. Wyatt was driven to succeed. At times that was his entire focus. At first Nora tried to understand, but as time went on, there was a growing resentment as she felt herself drop down the list of his priorities. She was good about telling him her feelings, but they just never seemed to stick. Wyatt acted like he heard her and then nothing changed.

Wyatt had a different perspective. He wondered where the compassionate, caring woman he'd fallen in love with had gone. She was distant, and while still an amazing mother, in his estimation she was failing him as a wife. She used to find ways to show him how much she cared, but it had been a long time since he'd received that attention.

They were drifting further and further apart. Even though they both looked great on the outside, the attraction was not the same. The inside changes affected the outside appearances. For the physical attraction to catch fire again, the internal work had to be done. As much emphasis as our culture puts on the outside, it is the inside attraction that makes a marriage awesome for a lifetime.

It's a truth that I learned early on as a counselor. A couple can look like they stepped out of a movie scene, but if things are not connecting internally, the outside makes no difference at all. A couple that is very average looking on the outside can be incredibly attracted to each other physically because the internal attributes continue to grow year after year. If you are going to work on attraction in your marriage, sure, stay as healthy as possible on the outside, but put your time, focus, and energy on being attractive inside. Grow those things that you saw in each other at the beginning and build new areas as God leads you. Remember, God will never do anything in your life that is not good for you, your spouse, and your marriage. Attraction goes so much deeper than the skin.

## THAT SPARK

Christopher: *"The spark is just not there anymore."*
Lilian: *"I still love him, just not that way anymore."*
Henry: *"The fire went out. I'm not sure we can ever get it going again."*

Samantha: *"He just sits in front of the TV. He never pays attention to me anymore. If he wanted to have sex, I don't know what I would do."*

Owen: *"She never puts in any effort to look good for me anymore. I'm not really attracted to her now."*

Scarlett: *"It feels weird when he touches me sexually now. I used to love his touch but not so much now."*

This list could go on and on. The spark of sexual energy between a couple can fizzle out if it is not nurtured. Unless there is betrayal, the spark usually goes out gradually. It's not like a couple has the spark one day and a few days later the spark is gone. The issue becomes a real problem when we ignore the warning signs, because the spark will begin to glow dimmer and dimmer until finally it goes out. Where is the sexual-energy spark between the two of you today? Where was it a year ago or five years ago? Never buy into the lie that the spark "just goes out." That is never true. The spark goes out because we do not tend it.

What are the warning signs? They can vary among couples, because every couple is unique. Every couple has a spark. Every couple knows what it was like when it burned the brightest for them. One couple's definition of "the brightest spark" in their marriage may be different than another couple's. Don't fall into the trap of comparison. What makes your spark a ten may be different from what Nancy and I would say is a ten for us or what your best friend would say was a ten for them. Spark comparison is a bad road to go down. Your ten is yours, and that is your standard. Stay focused on the two of you.

Now define your ten. Do this together. You will each have different things that go into your rating. That's okay. You are also different, beginning with the whole male and female thing, which is part of your uniqueness and part of what makes the spark such an awesome experience. Once you have your list of things that make the spark a ten for you, rate each of those things. If tenderness is on the list, rate how you are doing as a couple in this area. What did it look like when it was a ten? Where is it now? What can we do to close the gap? If flirtation is on the list, rate how you are doing as a couple in this area. What did it look like when it was a ten? Where is it now? What can you do to close the gap together? Now you have something concrete to work on. I suggest both of you focus on working on one thing at a time. Make sure you keep things balanced. If you work first on an area the wife brought up, then focus next on an area the husband brought up. I know this takes time, but, come on, you are igniting the spark! You should enjoy the process. Right?

Something that may interest you from my experience is that age does not seem to have a big effect on the spark. Sure, there is the hormone factor. These affect us sexually, both male and female, at different ages, but I think the spark is different. The spark is really an environment of sexual energy toward each other that does not always end in sex.

There was a guy who used to work for my dad when he owned supermarkets. This guy was awesome. I loved being around him. At ninety-two, he was full of passion and energy. I would work side by side with him on Saturdays when I was in high school. About an hour before he clocked out each week, he would begin to talk about his wife. The first time this happened, I thought he was married to some supermodel years younger than he was. He adored her inside and out. As quitting time approached that day, his wife came into the store to let him know she was there to pick him up. I saw her for the first time and then watched the two of them. They invented "spark." Their eyes locked, they smiled, he walked to her, kissed her, she laughed, and he laughed. As I looked at them, I realized everything he said about her was absolutely true. His description was perfect. I was able to see this amazing ninety-one-year-old woman through his eyes. I still remember thinking, *I so want that with someone one day.* That has been one of my goals since the day Nancy and I married. We work hard at keeping on that path, and "the spark" plays a big part in keeping us going.

A final thought on the spark. Whether yours is burning bright or has been out for too long, work on it. Whatever you need to do, work on it. Keep it burning bright. Relight it and keep it lit. It is truly one of the fun parts of an awesome marriage.

## REAL INTIMACY

When we look to the dictionary to help us define intimacy, there are a couple of ways we can go. The first seems to have crept into popular culture and focuses on the intimate act of sexual intercourse. For many people, intimacy equals sex. If a friend talks about intimacy with their spouse, we think of sex. When a couple comes to counseling to work on intimacy, at least one of them is focused on sex. Yet, intimacy is so much more than sex. It is a close familiarity or friendship between a husband and wife. That is the definition I want shouted from the tallest building in every town. Real intimacy is not sex. Can it lead to sex? Absolutely. The stronger the intimacy connection, the greater the potential for great sex, *but* intimacy itself is amazing.

Nancy and I know each other inside and out. We have studied each other for years. Sure, there are still some surprises, but we know each other on a deep intimate level. As we talked about in an earlier chapter, she is my best friend. Nancy and I have the intimate closeness between a husband and a wife. Go back to my ninety-two- and ninety-one-year-old couple. I don't know if they had sex or not, but they had intimacy.

For some people, real intimacy is enough. Maybe because of health issues or other problems, sex was off the table for a time, or for the rest of their lives. I have seen some of these couples who have so much more than a couple who just has sex. I'm not downplaying sex. You know from chapter 10 how I feel about sex. It is one of the most amazing gifts that God gives a couple to enjoy in marriage, but He also gives the gift of intimacy at a level in marriage that I don't think we can experience elsewhere in this life. What I want you to see is that sex and intimacy are different. Don't miss out on intimacy. The sex in my marriage is great because Nancy and I cultivated intimacy. In this chapter we have looked at flirting, nonsexual touching, attraction, and the spark. All of those are part of intimacy. You can do them anytime, anywhere and never get into trouble. Don't miss your opportunities for intimacy.

## KEYS TO INTIMACY

As we complete this chapter, here are some things I want you to think about:

- What does "close familiarity" look like for the two of you? How can you grow this area of your intimacy?
- We talked about friendship in an earlier chapter. When you think of your "close friendship" as a couple as it relates to intimacy, how are you doing? What would grow your "close friendship" to be more intimate?
- As you work on clarifying the difference between intimacy and sex in your marriage, separately write down three things you would like to be a part of each and then share your answers with each other.

*Going Deeper*

One of the things that helped Nancy and me was to take intimacy out of the bedroom. I know that sounds really strange, so let me explain. I think, like most couples, we put intimacy and sex in the same box. As we understood more about intimacy, we wanted to take it out of that box and have intimacy be a part of our lives 24/7/365. Sure, intimacy was still a part of sex in the bedroom, but intimacy was not sex. Discuss steps you can take together to cultivate a climate of 24/7/365 intimacy in your marriage.

# CHAPTER 12

# Distance: How to Bridge the Gap

## ANNA AND CALEB

For the fifteen years of their marriage, Caleb had been an amazing husband. His job had a lot of flexibility and always gave him the option of being available to Anna. They loved their time together. Anna's dad traveled a lot as Anna was growing up, and she often saw the sadness in her mom's face. His traveling brought challenges for the whole family. As her dad climbed up the corporate ladder, his traveling increased. For Anna, her dad's absence was her normal but as she entered her teen years, she began to empathize more and more with her mom. This was not what she wanted in her future marriage. Her dad's travel created distance between her parents, and it seemed as though her dad liked it that way. When he was home, he never made up for lost time with the family. Instead, he played golf, hung out with his friends, and would occasionally take the family to a movie.

As Anna compared her marriage to her parents', she saw so many differences. She and Caleb were connected in so many ways, which gave her security she felt her mom never had. The company Caleb worked for was growing, and he was a big part of the growth. The company was looking at expanding into another state, and if things came together, Caleb was their choice to launch the new office. The launch was projected to be a one-year process. After hours of wrestling with the options, Anna and Caleb decided that the best thing for the family was for Caleb to commute. He would fly out every Monday morning and return on Friday. They would Skype during the week and make the most of the weekends at home. After all, it was just for a year.

At first, Anna did well. The week went quickly as she adjusted to parenting alone part-time. About a month or so into their new normal, Anna suffered her first ever anxiety attack. The past weekend was full of "have tos," and she and Caleb had very little time together. Even when they had time, Caleb seemed distant. The daily Skype calls seemed shorter and again Caleb seemed preoccupied. Anna knew it was probably all in her head, but the fear of ending up like her mom scared her in a way she had never experienced before. The distance she felt involved a lot more than just the miles between them.

## WHERE ARE YOU?

There was a time when we did not have the technology of today. I was ecstatic when I purchased my Motorola flip phone. Many of you will have no idea what that is. That's okay. Someday your kids will have no idea about the things we think are so amazing today. Before cell phones, this was a common narrative. If someone called you, they *never* asked, "Where are you?" because they knew. You were on a landline tethered to your home, business, or some other place they had called. If you were driving around and wanted to call someone to say you were running late or just to check in, you had to locate a phone booth. A phone booth was the place where Clark Kent would change into the Man of Steel. As a mere human, you could step inside one, find a phone, pick it up, insert a few coins, and call someone. I learned all of this from watching old movies!

My point is this: Before cell phones, it took a lot of effort to connect with people. Even if you made the effort to call someone at home on their landline, there was no assurance that they were home. Before caller ID, you had no proof that you ever tried to call them. Today most of us have our phones in our hands, pockets, or purses. When someone calls, I know who is calling, and can choose not to answer. The problem is that the person calling knows what I did. One other side note. We have gone from the early years of using these cell phones exclusively for calls to mobile devices with so many uses that, for most of us, calling is the last thing we use them for.

That brings us to this dilemma. Technology has erased our excuses for not connecting. We have so many ways and so many options when it comes to connecting with another person. The expectation level has gone through the roof, and when we don't take advantage of the opportunities, the other person can feel neglected, rejected, and distant. The question for you is, as a couple, how can you use technology to bring you closer to each other and close the distance gap?

## JACK AND LUCY

I met Jack and Lucy when they came to see me about their teenage son. He was struggling in school, which was causing tension at home. They wanted me to help them come up with a plan to help their son and to help them deal with the situation. Great parents wanting to get ahead of any potential future problems. What I want to share with you had nothing to do with their counseling and everything to do with the way they leveraged technology for their marriage.

Let's take a look first at their mobile devices. Jack and Lucy both worked. Jack had a demanding full-time job that he loved. Lucy worked part-time on school days and also loved what she did. Jack got up early, worked out, and was sitting at his desk by seven thirty. Lucy was up at six thirty, had the kids out the door by seven thirty, and was off to work to be there a little before nine. Each day Lucy woke up to a Bitmoji from Jack. Sometimes they were sweet, sometimes funny, and sometimes sexy. Lucy would return the favor with a creative Bitmoji of her own. During the day they would text each other. The texts were not to get a conversation going but rather to let each other know they were thinking about the other. Jack did not travel much but when he did, they Skyped at night, sometimes for a few minutes and sometimes much longer. I asked them this question: "Do either of you ever feel distant from the other?" The answer from both was no. I believed them. If there were distance gaps between them, they both looked for ways to bridge the gaps. The were proactive with their marriage just like they were with their son.

## DANGER SIGNS

- Do you leave for hours or days at a time without explanation?
- Does your spouse leave for hours or days at a time without explanation?
- Have either of you lied about your whereabouts?
- Have either of you suspected the other was being unfaithful?
- Do either of you get angry when asked about your whereabouts?

Tough questions. Even tougher if you answer yes to one or more of them. We live in a society where trusting someone can be difficult. We all know someone who had a seemingly good marriage that ended abruptly. We know husbands and wives who have had affairs. Many of the people who get the most media coverage have no idea what a healthy relationship is. Hearing of someone being unfaithful who we never, ever thought would take that path can be devastating. We ask questions like, "Could it happen to us?" or "What happened to them?" or "Did they see it coming?" Red flags may pop up, but sometimes they're born out of our fears and aren't issues of unfaithfulness.

For example, a spouse who leaves for hours or days without explanation may not be having an affair but may be angry. An unexpected departure of a spouse is a sure sign of issues in the marriage, but not a sure sign of unfaithfulness. Stress does strange things to us, and changes in behavior can be one of them. A spouse under a lot of stress at work may become very distant at home and spend more time at work trying to reduce the stress. He or she is not having an affair even though some of the symptoms are similar. A couple who is consistently struggling with their sex life may wonder whether their spouse is being unfaithful if things are not getting better in this area of their marriage.

Lying is another example. Lying—for any reason—will cause mistrust. Maybe someone is just tired of his or her spouse's neediness and says what they want to hear to avoid an argument. It may stop the fight in the moment but it sets the stage for a potential war later on. When you don't trust your spouse, your mind can conjure up all kinds of unhealthy scenarios. Lying does not automatically equal an affair, but it is a marriage killer.

A spouse who constantly changes their mobile device or computer password may not be hiding anything, but this behavior can raise concern for their spouse if they went from being very open to suddenly seeming very private about everything. In other words, behaviors can mean many different things.

All are danger signs that need to be addressed because they will cause growing distance in a marriage. Many couples ignore the signs. Some are afraid of what the truth might be. Some assume it is temporary and will get better with time. Some are so caught up in the busyness of life that they hardly notice the distance in their marriage. None of these approaches work. Yes, the truth may hurt. It may be difficult to navigate. But fear will never solve the problem. Very few things in marriage work themselves out on their own. The distance created in a marriage from busyness will only continue to grow. At some point, one spouse may decide it is too much work to get things back on track.

What is your next step if you answered yes to one or more of the earlier questions? I believe in getting things out in the open where we can address them and begin to take the steps necessary to solve the problem. Is that a difficult step? Sure, but it is essential. Working on something today is better than tomorrow, next week, next month, or never. It is like getting the flu. If you start medication immediately, the illness will be far less severe. If you wait too long, the virus has set in and the medication is not nearly as effective.

## ELLIE AND CHARLES

Charles said that his marriage to Ellie had its up and downs from day one. He met her shortly after her divorce.

She said she was over her former spouse, but now he wondered if that was true. Was he a rebound who became a spouse? This was Charles's first marriage, and he had fallen in love with Ellie. Ellie seemed to care deeply for him, but he always felt there were some barriers between them. He hoped that time would draw them closer to each other. Ellie's first husband had been unfaithful, so Charles went out of his way to show he was a man she could trust. The first year of marriage was good, and Charles felt they were maybe beginning to close the distance gap.

About halfway through their second year of marriage, Charles felt Ellie pull away a little. At first he thought it was just his imagination and that things would get better. They did not. He picked up Ellie's phone to check the time and realized she had changed her password. They both had the same passwords on all their devices—it was the date he proposed. That code no longer opened her phone. Out of curiosity, he checked her email account and found that password was also changed. He was confused. Changing passwords was one of the things that tipped her off to her husband's affair. Was she doing the same thing? He couldn't go there, so for a while he did nothing. Then there seemed to be red flags everywhere. They had always talked with each other about their day. Now as they talked, there were gaps in Ellie's day. If he tried to get her to fill in the blanks, she became angry. Charles felt the signs were everywhere, and came to see me. I listened closely as he recounted the distance and changes in their marriage. He was sure she was having an affair but could not grasp the reality and what that meant for them. Why would she do to him what had been done to her? I asked Charles if he thought Ellie would talk to me. He was not sure but would ask her to call.

All the signs were there: secrecy, distance, changed passwords, and spans of time unaccounted for. All of these can go along with an affair, but not always. Fortunately for Charles and Ellie, that was not the case. Ellie had never really recovered from her divorce and the betrayal by her first husband. She poured herself into her marriage with Charles, but her fear of being hurt again eventually took over, and she put up walls everywhere she could. She even laughed a little at her actions, which were driven by some really crazy thoughts. Ellie thought that if she changed her passwords, Charles could not get information about her to plot his own affair. The gaps in her day were spent researching GPS trackers, cameras, and other things she could have on hand to protect herself if needed. Fear was ruling her life and driving a huge wedge between her and her husband. I asked her to share what she told me with Charles, and then we mapped out a plan for them. Ellie would see a female counselor to work through the issues she hadn't worked on before. I spent time with them on marriage issues and building the marriage that they both wanted.

Distance is a red flag that cannot be ignored. Whatever the reason for the distance, there is always an answer. Is there distance between you and your spouse today? Are you avoiding working on it? Will you commit to put it all on the table and begin the healing process?

### RELIEF

So far we have talked about the red flags that indicate there is distance in a marriage. A spouse will feel the effects, know something is wrong, and hopefully address the issue. But what about a spouse who loves the distance? This person is relieved when their spouse goes out of town or calls to say they will be home late. The husband has been snoring and his wife is secretly happy when he moves to the other room to sleep. In each scenario, one spouse considers the distance a welcome reprieve. They see their spouse as a dark cloud and cannot wait until that cloud moves away.

For me, these situations are really sad. A couple that once had the potential of an awesome marriage has settled into a life of isolation. It is like a basketball team with several good players who won't share the ball. One player ignores his teammates time after time, going down the court so he can take the shot. "Iso ball" is what it's called. Just like isolation in marriage, it may work for a time but it is never the best solution. If the basketball player is on a hot shooting streak, iso ball may work, but what about the game when his shots are not dropping at all? It's the same in marriage. Iso ball may bring temporary relief, but what about the dream of having a great marriage? Where does that go?

If you feel relief when your spouse is gone, is late, or

always sleeps in the other room, that's a problem. It is far from God's plan: remember the whole idea of "two become one" or "two are better than one"? It's time to address the problem. Most likely it has gone on for a long time if you are feeling relief. Maybe both of you feel relief.

Step one is to agree that you are settling for something that does not resemble marriage. You may have a piece of paper that says you are man and wife, but when you put your marriage next to God's design, what does it look like?

Step two is getting help. Most couples are not going to overcome this on their own. Find a good Christian counselor. Then, ask people you trust to pray for you and hold you both accountable to do what the counselor tells you to do.

Step three requires you to push through when the going gets rough—because there is a good chance it will. Change is difficult, but perseverance will get your marriage to where you want it to be.

And finally, celebrate along the way. When your spouse leaves the house and you miss them, tell them. When you realize you really missed sleeping side by side, even with the CPAP machine, tell them. Bottom line: Don't settle. Life is too short and God's plan for marriage is too precious.

## PHYSICAL VERSUS EMOTIONAL

For most of us, both the physical and emotional distance can cause problems. The physical distance takes many forms. A couple may be apart for a night, a week, or longer. Each has its own challenges. Maybe you think that a night apart is not a big deal. I agree. But what if you used that night as an opportunity to grow your marriage? Think about what you could do while away that would let your spouse know they are still at the top of your list. I know a wife whose husband travels, so she always has a note waiting for him when he checks into a hotel. Think about what that does for the husband. He knows she took the time to do something special for him. It connects them in a special way even though they may be miles apart. Her husband told me that it never gets old.

Other times of separation have their own challenges, but technology can bring us together no matter how many miles are between us. Nancy and I know a couple who is going through a year apart while he is deployed. This is his third deployment during their marriage. It is never easy, but they leverage technology and stay in close contact. Is it the same as being face-to-face? No, but it's so much better than pre-technology days.

When I think about my parents' early years of marriage, I can't even comprehend all they endured. My dad was gone for months at a time fighting a war in another part of the world. They bridged the distance with snail-mail letters. I have a trunk full of them; he wrote my mother almost every day that he was gone. They used what they had to close the distance. Today we have so many ways to connect that distance becomes a problem only if we let it. Being proactive to connect closes the gap. What if military couples don't take advantage of what is available to connect them? What if a couple never connects when they are apart for a night, a few days, or weeks?

Are the two of you ever separated by physical distance? How do you handle the time apart? Do you find ways to connect and remain closely tied to each other's lives? What could you do to close the gap when the two of you are apart?

While we may anticipate some challenges with physical distance, we don't expect to encounter emotional distance. We are marrying the person of our dreams. Our Prince Charming. Our beautiful bride. We are supposed to live happily ever after, and happily ever after includes being emotionally connected. Emotional distance is different. You can be sitting side by side in your home and feel apart. The plan is for that emotional connection to grow and deepen over the years of a marriage. Sadly, for some it never grows. When that connection does not happen and expectations are not met, the emotional distance begins. So when emotional distance rears its ugly head in marriage, we don't know what to do. We may say something like, "I don't feel as close to you as I used to." That's a pretty vulnerable statement. It is a stretch for many people to even get those words out. Then, if the receiving spouse blows it off or discounts it in any way, the other spouse will usually either fight back in an unhealthy way or withdraw. Now the emotional distance grows and the spouse who took the risk will be very cautious about bringing up the problem again. One wife told me that she'd never felt as lonely as she did sitting beside her husband. I believe that most couples have an emotional connection at some time in their relationship.

On the other hand, if the receiving spouse says, "Me too," or, "I don't want you to feel that way. What can I do to help?" the emotional gap begins to close. The longer the emotional distance goes unattended, the more difficult the process of repair and healing.

Have the two of you ever experienced emotional distance? Was there a catalyst that led to the distance? How can you keep from repeating that pattern? Has the emotional distance resulted in physical distance? What can each of you do to begin connecting again?

## CAMERON AND SARAH

Cameron and Sarah were celebrating their seventeenth wedding anniversary. It was a big party. A joy-filled celebration. Five years earlier, no one believed they would make it through the year. Previously they fought a lot and never really resolved anything. There were good things in their marriage, and they both loved their three kids. Parenting together was never an issue for them. They just had trouble living under the same roof. Cameron would leave for days and stay with a single buddy. He was still there to help with the kids and provide for Sarah. They even had a weekly date night that they both looked forward to. The nights away were increasing, and Sarah told her mom that their marriage seemed to be better like this. As Cameron drove onto their street one day, he noticed the home across the street was for sale. What if he bought that home? He and Sarah could live across the street from each other, and the kids could go back and forth anytime they wanted. They could have the physical distance they both needed. Surprisingly, Sarah liked the plan and in thirty days they became across-the-street neighbors. Five years later they were still married and the celebration was on.

Some of you may be thinking, *That's not a bad idea. If we could afford it, that might be a solution for us too.* The main reason I tell this story is that I see other Camerons and Sarahs doing the same thing. Couples who stay married and live separately. Before we go any further, I need to say that I think this is a terrible idea. Let's look at this together:

- Cameron and Sarah never gave counseling a chance. They came up with a solution that stopped the fighting but never solved their issues. They just avoided them. That is never healthy for a marriage.
- Cameron and Sarah really could not afford two houses. They sacrificed a lot to make it work and had zero extra money to do the things they dreamed of doing as a family.
- They were the up-close marriage model for their kids. Is that what they wanted for their kids when they married?
- Trust was not broken between them, but there were a lot more questions about faithfulness as they lived apart.

- Just because something "works" does not mean that it resolves anything.
- The distance they had living in two houses was a bandage at best.
- One year to the day after their youngest child graduated from high school, Cameron and Sarah were divorced.
- When the bandage was ripped off, all the problems were still there.

Distance and technology: more ways to keep up with each other than any generation has ever had before; more ways to connect; more ways to express love; more ways to close the physical and emotional distance gaps. Distance can make or break a marriage. What about your marriage? Is it a distance maker or a distance breaker?

## KEYS TO BRIDGING THE GAP

As we complete this chapter, here are some things I want you to think about:

- What are your expectations of each other as far as using technology to close distance gaps?
- As a couple, what are ways that you can be proactive with technology in your marriage?
- What do you need to watch for that could be red flags for you in your marriage? How could you address these with each other?

*Going Deeper*

Depending on your stage of marriage, what are the danger areas for each of you when it comes to emotional distance? How can you address these red flags with each other before they become more severe issues? When coming up with solutions for your marriage, what are the dangers of leaving God out?

# CHAPTER 13

# Role Models: What Did You See?

With over 50 percent of first marriages ending in divorce, many people did not have both parents in the home as they grew up. Statistically a lot of people enter marriage with very little role modeling that will help them have a successful marriage. As a counselor, I see many people whose parents left a lot to be desired. Yet we know that our own parents are our textbook for what it looks like to be a mother or father, wife or husband, woman or man. There are so many things that affect the roles we see our parents play in our formative years.

Growing up, I had a number of men who influenced my life, but the model in front of me day after day was my dad. Most of what I knew about women and the roles they play came from my mother. She was there every day. The same is true for you. Even if your parent was present only a very little, or not at all, that influenced how you view that parent's role. If your dad was not around, you may see a father's role as someone who is absent, untrustworthy, or uncaring. If your parents were divorced, they may have done a great job as a mom and a dad, but you didn't get to see them interact daily in the same home.

Yet that is not the entire problem. We cannot help what happened with our parents. We had very little control, if any, over how they parented, treated each other, or acted as man and woman. We do have control over what we do with the information we observed. We can say, "My parents loved me but they were not very good role models for marriage. If I model my marriage after theirs, there is a good chance mine will not be the marriage I dreamed of and a good chance it will fail just like theirs did." Awareness is one thing; action is another. We can have all the awareness in the world and not make a change. If we want a different outcome, we have to be very intentional in writing a different script for our marriage daily.

## JONATHAN AND KAYLEE

Jonathan was only five when his parents divorced. He doesn't remember much about those first five years of his life but does remember his parents yelling and that after his dad moved out, their home was really quiet. His mom started a new job. It was her first job in his life since having him. That fall Jonathan started an all-day kindergarten program at the neighborhood school and then went to an after-school program until his mom picked him up. Jonathan's dad was great with visitation and never was late or missed the chance to spend time with his son. They were close when Jonathan was five and remained close through his high school years. His dad dated a number of different women that Jonathan never met, and he did not remarry until Jonathan was in college. His mother, on the other hand, remarried when Jonathan was seven. Landon was nice enough but was very focused on his work. He told Jonathan that he would be there if needed but wasn't about to take on the role of a father. He didn't have time for that. Besides, Landon said, "You have a great dad." That was certainly true and made sense to Jonathan. At first his mom seemed very happy, but over the next couple of years that changed. His mom and Landon never fought, which was great, but they didn't seem to be very close either. When he was a teenager, Jonathan asked his mom if she was happy in her marriage with Landon. She said, "Landon is a fine man and provides really well for us. His work is very important to him."

Kaylee was two years younger than Jonathan. Looking back, she knew that her parents struggled financially for years. They had a small two-bedroom home for the family, which included Kaylee's brother, who was a year older. Over the next few years, Kaylee's dad gradually went from an associate in a big law firm to owner of his own firm with a number of attorneys on staff. They moved from the small home to a much, much bigger one. Kaylee said, "As much as I enjoyed the big home and getting a brand-new car on my sixteenth birthday, we were happiest as a family in the little house. I wish that things had never changed."

She remembered great family times and watching her mom and dad enjoy each other. They all had fun together. As her dad's career grew, there was less time at home. Her mom took on many of the roles her dad had played. Her parents seemed to be drifting apart and the fun family times did not exist. After moving to the new home, they were like four people living separate lives. She and her brother stayed in their large rooms with every teenage comfort imaginable. Her mom was either in her study or the parents' bedroom. On many mornings she found her dad asleep in his recliner in the den with the TV still on. She wanted to find a college that was as far away from home as she could get.

By telling their stories and listening to them again in my office, Jonathan and Kaylee gained some new awareness of why their marriage was struggling. Jonathan loved Kaylee and was a great dad. The dad part seemed to come easy for him, and he gave his own dad most of the credit. As a husband, Jonathan did not score nearly as high. He started off well, happy to be close to Kaylee, but when the newness of marriage wore off, he was not sure what to do, so he did exactly what his dad had done. He worked really hard and spent most of his time away from work being a father. Kaylee was usually there, too, but the focus was on the kids. Somewhere in the back of his mind was the thought, *When the kids leave, maybe Kaylee and I can spend more time together.*

The more Jonathan worked to provide, the more the fear rose in Kaylee. Was she repeating her parents' path? When she tried to talk to Jonathan about her concerns, he listened, but nothing ever changed. She found herself doing exactly what she saw her mom do: nothing. She enjoyed the fruits of his labors, put time into being a mom, and put her marriage dreams on the back burner. Jonathan and Kaylee did not give up, and divorce for them was never on the table. They would just exist as they were, and maybe someday things would get better. They chose a solution that was not really a solution at all.

There are thousands and thousands of Jonathans and Kaylees out there. The details of the story may change, but the core problem of not knowing how to be a husband and a wife is the same. Other couples also choose to stay together for a number of different reasons. Then there are many couples that make different decisions, ranging from affairs to divorce. So many people lack good role models for marriage. It takes a lot of work to break that cycle. It starts with an awareness of the void in your life and then taking responsibility to change. You won't learn to be a great husband or wife by standing around doing nothing. It's something to work on individually and as a couple. Not only will your marriage become something you cherish, but you will be writing a textbook for your children that you will be ecstatic for them to read.

LEADING

I listen to a couple of leadership podcasts regularly and read leadership books. I want to be the best leader of Awesome

Marriage. Leading my team, investing in them, and seeing them succeed are constant goals. I think I do a good job most of the time. Getting positive feedback as I lead motivates me to keep getting better.

The Bible tells me that I am supposed to be the leader of my home and marriage. There are podcasts and books on this, but all too often they get moved down in my queue. Why is it so difficult for men to lead their wives? Do our wives even *want* to be led? These two questions have been around a long time. When Jesus spoke about leadership, He was speaking to the audience in front of Him and to generations yet to come. The issues and problems in culture then, in many ways, mirror ours today. Marriages were in trouble. Husbands were not leading, and wives did not trust their husbands to lead. Sound familiar?

Since God's word never changes, it is worth our time to revisit some of these passages and see what we can learn and apply to our lives today. In Mark 10:43–45, Jesus says these words: "But among you it will be different. Whoever wants to be a leader among you must be your servant, and whoever wants to be first among you must be the slave of everyone else. For even the Son of Man came not to be served but to serve others and to give His life as a ransom for many" (NLT). Well, that is pretty tough definition. This is what I hear Jesus saying:

- You need to be different from the others out there.
- To be a leader you must serve those you are leading.

- Jesus came to serve us.
- As a servant, Jesus gave His life for us.

For me, then, my definition of leading Nancy is to serve her and to lay my own desires aside to put hers first. I can hear some of you now: "That's not fair." I couldn't agree more, but it was also not fair for Jesus to serve me to the point of losing His life. Leading as a husband is a really big deal and one that God takes very seriously.

This is the point where, as men, we say something like, "Not only is it unfair, but also I can never measure up and do this right. I am doomed to failure as a husband." Aren't you glad you decided to read this chapter? Realistically, that line of thinking is true for us because we know on our own we will never measure up. The good news is that we are not alone! God never gives us a task that He will not equip us to do. Can you imagine Moses leading the Israelite people out of Egypt without God's help? Could Moses have parted the Red Sea on his own? What about Paul? Here we have a man who hated and murdered Christians and whom God turned into the greatest missionary and evangelist ever. If God can do that with these men, think what He can do with you as He teaches you to lead your family!

I want to camp out on Jesus' words a little longer and share with you what God has taught and continues to teach me. First, my biggest issue was, and still is, my own selfishness. That is a problem. It becomes an even bigger problem when it comes to being a servant. If I am to serve Nancy like God wants me to, it means that she comes before me *and* (this is the really hard and really important part) I am to like it. I need to be joyful as I serve her, not angry or begrudging. Yuck! So, are there times when I serve her well because that is what God wants me to do? Yes. God wants me to be a consistent servant. And doing what God wants me to do will eventually bring *me* joy, apart from what it does for my marriage.

Still have questions? Here are some ways I think God has led me to serve Nancy:

- I pray each day that God will help me to love her the way He wants me to love her.
- I look for ways to make her day easier.
- I ask her how I can help her.
- I pray with and for her.
- I do YouVersion reading plans with her.
- I sometimes do her chores for her.
- I listen to her when she is talking to me.
- I compromise.

In most of our marriages, when we consistently serve our wives, they in turn want to love us better—but that is not the point. No matter how Nancy responds, God still wants me to be obedient to Him and serve her. For some of you, your spouse may not respond the way you would like, but I promise you that there is real joy in being obedient to God. How would you rate yourself as a leader in your marriage today? Ask your wife how she would rate you. As you look at both ratings, how are you doing? Most of us are going to see a need for improvement. Don't get overwhelmed. Take it a step at a time. Start with prayer. Ask God to equip you to be the leader that He wants you to be in your marriage. Ask Him to soften your heart and give you the heart of a servant like Jesus was talking about. When you take that first step, you will find a loving God waiting for you.

## BEING LED

Ladies, if your husband is to be the leader God wants him to be, he has to have someone to lead—and that is you! Now it's your turn to be scared! I am kidding, but I know from talking to many wives that letting your husband lead may be frightening for you. Maybe you tried to let him lead in the past. Maybe you wanted him to lead, and he failed or let you down. Maybe you have decided it is easier to do marriage without his leadership. Maybe for whatever reason (and it may be a very valid reason), you do not trust him to lead. I get all of that. I also know that God still wants him to lead, and if your husband has a renewed commitment to lead in your marriage, the only wife he has to lead is you! No one can give him that opportunity but you. Plus, your role in this is essential. Not only is it important for you to let him lead, your feedback to him in a loving way is something God will use as He is molding your husband. Think about what that alone can do for your marriage. You, your husband, and God all working together in this—is awesome!

Here are some things for you to consider:

- Ask God to open your heart to see what He is doing in your husband.
- Give your fears and anxieties to God.
- Encourage your husband as he seeks to be a godly leader.
- Give feedback gently and with encouragement.
- Rejoice in what God is doing.

## GRAD SCHOOL

My college life as an undergraduate was about as different as possible from my life as a graduate student. I attended TCU as a freshman with a business management major. My granddad and my dad were both in the supermarket business under the family name. It seemed only natural that I would carry on the tradition. My priorities in college were twofold: first, have fun, and second, get an education. My priorities were backward. The summer before my senior year, I needed to go to summer school to make sure I had enough credits to graduate on time, in four years. My dad thought that four years of partying was enough.

After graduation, I went to work for my dad and settled into that role. A few years later, I knew God was calling me to something else, but I wasn't sure what that would be. Over the next few years, God patiently led me to where He wanted me to be, and I enrolled in graduate school. The consequences of too much fun at TCU came back to bite me, and I entered grad school on probation. I had one semester to prove myself. This was different. This time God was involved and He was calling me to be full-time for Him. I got the priorities right this time. I worked hard and learned everything I could. I felt like a sponge soaking everything up. I loved it, and my grades reflected that love. Everything that I thought about doing academically as an undergraduate I did in grad school. I was a different student with different priorities and a different motivation. It was an amazing time in my life.

In many ways, understanding our roles as a husband and a wife can be similar to that college versus grad school experience. College was the time you spent growing up in your family home. That's where you first learned about roles and your first definition of a husband and a wife. Since most of us had a few gaps in this education, we entered grad school, or marriage, with more to learn. With two master's degrees and two doctorates, I spent a lot of years in grad school.

As you enter the grad school of role models, plan to stay a lifetime. Don't let that frustrate you. I have discovered that I will always be working on my role as a husband to Nancy. Some of that is because I can be a slow learner in certain areas, and the rest is because people and needs can change over time. In many ways, what

Nancy needs from me today is different from what she needed a few years ago. Today we are not raising a family and we have more time for each other. Knowing that her love language is quality time gives me the opportunity to focus on quality time without some of the distractions I had in the past. The essential role of being a leader does not change.

Whatever your family of origin looked like, you are responsible for your marriage and family today. Your role as a husband or a wife is yours to define and learn with God's guidance. I have never counseled a person who did not want to be the spouse God designed them to be. They see the value but just need a road map to get there.

Let's look at some ideas:

- Make two lists relating to your family of origin. On one list, write down everything you valued in your family that you think God would have you bring forward into your marriage. On the other list, write down everything from your family that you think God would have you leave behind. Use these lists as checkpoints as you each seek to improve your roles in your marriage.

- Work together on role goals for each of you as a husband and a wife. Support each other in the process and pray for each other.

- This will be an evolving process, so update your list every year. For example, one year may have more time for you to pray and study the Bible together than you had in the past.

- Celebrate your successes along the way!

We all have a choice. We can repeat the bad patterns set by our parents or do something different. Which do you choose?

## THREE REPEATS

### Aaron and Kennedy

Aaron's dad was abusive. Most of it was verbal, but a couple of times he saw his dad hit his mom. It was always that way. Yelling, screaming, blaming, and then slamming the door loudly on his way out. Aaron hated it. When Aaron was young, his hate was directed at his dad. As he grew older, he hated his dad's words and actions. Aaron saw some of the same behavior in his granddad. His mother said it used to be a lot worse, but his granddad had mellowed over time. When he turned eighteen, Aaron confronted his dad and told him if it did not stop, he would stop it. As far as Aaron knew, it stopped. But he also knew that once he drew the line in the sand, his mother would never tell him if his dad crossed it.

Kennedy was so much like his mother. Aaron heard that people marry people like their opposite-sex parent, but he never put much credence in it. Now it kind of made sense. Aaron loved his mother deeply and celebrated all she had done for him. He always wondered how much better his mother would have been with a husband who loved and cherished her. Aaron vowed to love Kennedy that way, and for a long time he did. Then one day after he came home from work, Kennedy confronted him with something she discovered that he was ashamed of. Enter his dad. It was like he was standing outside of his own body watching this monster explode but unable to do anything about it. He was doing to Kennedy what his dad did to his mom and his granddad did to his grandmother. He was part of this generational curse and had no idea how far back it went.

Yet there was a difference. Aaron reached out for help. He called his pastor, talked to every man in his small group, started Christian counseling, enrolled in an anger management class, and did everything else anyone suggested. His new motto was "This stops here."

### Katherine and Parker

Katherine's dad was pretty passive and her mother was very strong. Some people thought she was a control freak. Maybe she was. Katherine just thought, "That's the way Mom is," and she was used to it. Her dad was gentle with her, very loving, a good provider for the family (although her mom said that she also had to work if they were going to have anything extra), and very soft spoken. Her mom ruled the home and her dad seemed fine with it. Katherine thought she did a really good job. Her parents never fought, and she felt they had a system that worked well for them. She never thought about how that might affect her later in life.

Katherine and Parker met at a mutual friend's Super Bowl party. They were the only two there rooting for a certain team and bonded over that likeness. Parker reminded her of her dad in many ways. He, too, was gentle and caring and had a good job. When she saw her dad and Parker together, she realized he was a much stronger personality than her dad. She liked that about him. Katherine and Parker got engaged after dating for almost three years. They were both almost thirty and saw no need for premarital counseling. They would be just fine.

When you come into marriage without ever talking about how you will handle things and who will do what, you will often find yourself in conflict. Katherine and Parker fell into this category. After only a few months of marriage, Parker saw a side of Katherine that he never knew existed. She was trying to control everything. Katherine, on the other hand, could not believe that Parker would not let her take care of things like her mom did for her dad. The marriage went from bliss to "what did I get myself into?" fairly quickly. They agreed to counseling without any concept of the baggage they would bring into the counseling room.

### Gavin and Bella

Gavin and Bella both grew up in divorced homes. Gavin was ten when his parents called it quits. The morning after Gavin heard his parents fighting into the night, his dad came into his room and told Gavin that he was leaving. That fight the night before started when his parents disagreed on how to discipline Gavin for an incident. It escalated into a number of unresolved issues, but Gavin blamed himself. "If I had not gotten in trouble, Dad would not be leaving."

Bella was fourteen when her parents divorced. They never fought in front of Bella, and she was shocked when they said they were splitting. Her dad moved to another home and her parents agreed to fifty-fifty visitation. Not long after the divorce, Bella's mom introduced Bella to her new boyfriend. For Bella, the pieces of the divorce began to fit together.

Bella and Gavin were good friends in high school and knew pieces of each other's story. When Bella ran for senior class president, Gavin managed her victorious campaign. Neither wanted to go to college. Gavin's dad was an electrician and had a great business. He invited Gavin to come and learn the trade. If he liked it, he could become a partner. Bella went to beauty school and loved the idea of helping women look their best. Neither really dated much and they seemed to keep bumping into each other. Finally, Gavin asked her out. Bella said yes and in eighteen months they were married.

I was their premarital counselor, and a number of red flags popped up as we talked. I told them that there was nothing to keep them from getting married but that I wanted their commitment to continue counseling after the wedding. They agreed, and a month later we began to dig into issues that went back a long time for both of them.

As we wrap up this chapter, here are a couple of things for you to consider. First, no one grew up in a perfect family.

Most parents try really hard, but their effectiveness depends on whether or not they have dealt with their baggage. Second, you can either break the cycle or carry it on. If you choose to break the cycle, God will do amazing things. He will honor your choice and give you an awesome marriage.

## KEYS TO MOVING PAST
## YOUR ROLE MODELS

As we complete this chapter, here are some things I want you to think about:

- How healthy or unhealthy were the role models you saw in your family of origin?
- Do you see yourself repeating unhealthy patterns that were modeled for you? What are they?
- How will you pursue fulfilling the role God has given you in your marriage?

*Going Deeper*

What is an unhealthy cycle from your family of origin that you want to break? Make a plan together to break this cycle and leave a new legacy for your children.

# CHAPTER 14

# That Other Thing in Your Life: The Internet

The *Cambridge Dictionary* defines the internet as "the large system of connected computers around the world that allows people to share information and communicate with each other." Today we can access vast amounts of information, resources, and services. The world is truly at our fingertips. For someone like me who loves to do research, the internet and all it offers is amazing. In just a few seconds, I have information that would have taken many hours or days to find pre-internet. I am a huge fan.

In 2007, I first connected with people struggling with marriage issues through the internet while helping with Life.Church Online. Out of that experience Awesome Marriage was born. It just made sense to bring marriage help to where we found the most people: online. With the constant development of new technology, doors are always opening, giving us new, innovative ways to reach people with God's plan for marriage. If I were to list every way we use the internet today in our everyday lives, it would be somewhat outdated by the time you read this.

Think about the positive ways the internet helps your lives as a husband and a wife. Email communication cut out the middle man. You can send information to your spouse and they receive it immediately. For those who travel or are away from each other for whatever reason, email allows for instant communication. We have access to more entertainment now than we could possibly consume in a thousand lifetimes. Online shopping continues to grow, giving us access to stores and products instantly. That perfect gift for your spouse can be found online in just a few minutes and show up at your door in a few hours or a few days. Budgeting for a couple is easier than ever with online banking and financial services. A couple can study and learn about any and every subject. The Bible, as well as ways to study and read it together, is available in numerous formats. You two can play your favorite love song anytime you want to hear it. You can probably think of many other things to add to this list. My point is that the internet adds value to our lives and our marriages in so many ways.

Then there are the negatives. It seems that for everything that has a positive there is also a negative. I really hate that. For some reason, we can take something good and find a way to use it for bad. We cannot leave things alone. We have to change things, and that goes all the way back to Adam and Eve. The problems that these negatives cause us in our lives and in our marriages vary. The gamut runs from irritating to devastating. Let's look at some of them.

**Time.** Time is precious, and we talk about how important it is to be intentional in how we spend it. With the fascination and wealth of information on the internet, it is easy to get totally immersed in it at the expense of time with your spouse. If Nancy says, "Dinner will be ready in about forty-five minutes. Let's sit down and talk about our day before we eat," I have a choice. I can continue doing what I am doing on the internet or log off and be with her. I have a few seconds to make that decision. If I don't log off right then, my tendency is to get refocused on the computer, and once I do that, the forty-five minutes will fly by. Then I have created a problem by sending the message that whatever I am doing is more important than Nancy. That is not the message I wanted to send.

**Money.** With all the online stores that offer everything we ever wanted, needed, desired, or dreamed of, the temptation to buy and overspend is real. It's so easy to see something that just a few minutes ago we did not know we needed and add it to our cart. If you are like me, once it is in my cart, it is really hard to take back out. So, as a couple, you agree to a new budget. There is money in the budget for you to spend as you want, but the item in your cart goes over that amount. Now you have a decision to make. Cart or budget? If the budget wins, no problem. Once the impulse subsides, we are usually okay with not buying something. If the cart wins, then there is a problem. The ease and comfort of buying online is great until we cross a line that we agreed not to cross.

**Porn.** I talk about the problem of porn so much that I am going to say only one thing about it here. If it is not stopped, porn will eventually kill your marriage one way or another. If you don't believe me, keep it up. I try really hard to never say, "I told you so," but I told you so.

**Other people.** According to a recent article I saw, the internet is now the number three place affairs start, following the workplace and the gym. From my experience in the past few years, I would put it at number two, with the workplace being number one. Yet, even when it begins in the workplace, the affair often grows through online contact. I don't blame the internet. People have been having affairs since biblical times. People will continue to have affairs until time ends. I just don't want it to be you.

## TAYLOR AND COOPER

Taylor and Cooper met through friends over Christmas break one year. Over the next couple of years they stayed in touch. Cooper moved to the West Coast to begin his career after receiving a good offer from a great company. Taylor remained in Fort Worth. She was in a job she loved and saw no reason to move. This relationship was just beginning, and she had no idea where it was going. It did go— forward. Trips to and from the West Coast became more frequent, and both were getting a clearer picture of where this was heading. They loved each other but knew a decision was coming. You can date long-distance for a while, but marriage long-distance is never an option.

I was honored when they asked me to do their wedding and their premarital counseling. They loved the format of meeting up with me online for our pre-marriage sessions. Each week they would watch one of my videos online, and then we would meet for an hour through an online platform. We worked on all the basics, from communication and conflict resolution to sex and their spiritual relationship together. Yet there was the elephant in the room from the beginning. Where would they live? I decided to let that lie for a while. This was the first time I had attempted to counsel a couple online as they prepared for marriage. It worked really well. It was literally like the three of us were sitting together in my office. Sometimes in the counseling process timing is everything. Not my timing, but God's. My job is to wait on Him.

Looking back, I can see the foundation we were laying for their future marriage was the key to resolving where they would live. Finally, our last session came, and it was time to deal with the elephant. They listened to each other. They looked at options together. Finally, they came up with a compromise that worked for both of them. They would live the first two years of their marriage on the West Coast. During that time, Cooper would go through the process of relocating with another company in Fort Worth. Taylor was able to transfer to another office on the West Coast with her company with the promise of getting her old position back in two years. The elephant disappeared. It was a win for each of them and for their marriage.

This is what I learned. Counseling online works. There were none of the barriers that I thought might be there.

It opened my eyes to the possibilities of helping couples in new ways. As I look through the Bible, I see God meeting His people in different places under different circumstances. He still does that today. The internet is just another way for Him to work.

## STORIES

This story has thousands of faces. It is played out in every state multiple times every day. It begins with a click and often ends in bed. In my opinion, it is the single most destructive thing a married person can do online. It begins with curiosity. What if? What if I found that person I used to like? What if I send a personal email to that person in the office? What if we just started talking online? Click. Click. Click. As you are reading this, someone is making the decision to click.

## KEVIN AND LYDIA

Two babies in two years was overwhelming for Kevin. It wasn't that he didn't love them. He did. He really did, but they took a lot of time and energy, and Lydia was always exhausted. Many nights she slept in the rocking chair with one of the babies. Both children had allergies and other health issues. Kevin could not remember when they were both healthy at the same time. It had to be a long time ago. Kevin volunteered to be on the committee for his high school reunion. It would be a few meetings and then helping contact class members. At the second meeting, there were lists of "lost classmates" to track down. When he picked up the list with Julia Nolen's name on it, his first instinct was to get another list, but he never put it down. Julia was the girl he thought he would marry, but Julia was not on the same page with him, and after graduation they went separate ways. Now no one knew where she lived.

Lydia went to a different high school and had never met Julia. She knew Julia was one of Kevin's old girlfriends but Kevin never filled in the blanks for her. So when Kevin told Lydia about the meeting and showed her the list of people he was in charge of tracking down, Lydia said nothing as she scanned the list. That weekend while Lydia and the babies were napping, Kevin began his search. Julia was about halfway down his list and he moved her to the top. He ran all the searches he could think of and never found the right Julia Nolen. He was amazed that there were so many Julia Nolens. At church that Sunday, he ran into Thomas, who was also on the committee. He shared with Thomas that Julia seemed to have fallen off the face of the earth. Thomas looked puzzled and then said, "I think I heard somewhere that she started going by her middle name when she moved away after graduation. I think it was Hadley." During nap time after church that afternoon, Kevin was back online and there she was. Hadley Nolen. He sent her a message and waited. Nothing. Then two days later there was a message back. Kevin was connected to Hadley Nolen and no one would suspect anything. He was just doing his job for the reunion. His old feelings for her came back like a flood, and he could tell she was feeling something too.

There were so many times when Kevin could have said no, but he didn't. He knew he was vulnerable. He knew even getting on the committee was a bad idea for him with his marriage in a rocky place. He knew when he picked up the list with her name on it that he should have set it down and picked a different one. He knew not finding her at first was a great opt out. He knew all of that—but still moved forward. Click after click after click.

### QUINN AND HUDSON

Quinn was mortified when her best friend, Alyssa, revealed that she was on a dating site. Alyssa was married and had children. She told Quinn that she was just curious and it was harmless. She would never respond to anyone and felt safe because she used a false identity. Besides, there were other women doing it, and it was really nice to be pursued again. That night, Quinn started to tell Hudson about Alyssa but decided not to.

Over the next couple of weeks, Quinn could not get the idea of the dating site out of her head. It was harmless and Hudson had quit pursuing her after the first baby. No one would know, and it would be nice to see if other men found her attractive. Click. The profile was done and uploaded and now she was on the site. After a couple of days, she thought she'd made a big mistake. There were no lookers or takers. She needed to take down her profile before she felt worse. As she went online, there was a message. It was from a guy who saw her picture and he said she was beautiful. So much for taking down the profile. This felt good. It was not every day, but there were more guys saying more nice things. She felt better about herself than she had in a long time and was convinced that she was doing nothing wrong. No one knew. She didn't even tell Alyssa.

It seems that people can play with matches for only so long before one ignites. First the spark and then the fire. Quinn had the matches in her hands for a really long time. Then one day there was a spark and later there was the fire. She was constantly online checking for an email or a message or some other communication from him. He kept pressing her to meet him. She kept making up excuses. Finally there was a day that she did not have an excuse and the fire was out of control. It started with a click. So seemingly innocent. She would give anything to be able to take it back but it was too late. Too late for her, for Hudson, and for her kids.

## ISABELLA AND JORDAN

It seems that a lot of people travel for their work. It's so easy to leave on an early morning flight, arrive at your destination, do a day of business, and be home that same evening.

That was Jordan's routine. He traveled three days a week, and Isabella loved the schedule. He was home every night. So Jordan's problem did not start because he was doing overnights in some hotel halfway across the country. He had his safeguards in place. Day trips were no different than leaving for the office in the morning, working all day, and coming home at night. Jordan landed a new account that was going to require some extra work, but the potential payout for him was really good.

For the next six weeks, he would travel every day. It was going to be the same office in the same city, but he was determined to be home at night and he was. A number of things happened during those six weeks that led to a problem. Even though he was home at night, he was getting tired. The travel was wearing on him. Isabella was busy with her home business and the kids and checked out of the marriage for a while. It was not a conscious decision but seemed okay to her given the circumstances of their lives at that time. Jordan was meeting with the same person each day: an attractive, recently divorced woman about his age. He first saw her as a business acquaintance. She was key to the success of the project. The truth was that she was not looking either; her divorce was painful. But when you work side by side with someone day after day and your only constraint is going home at night, eventually, it is not enough. This relationship began in an office and blossomed online. There were messages, emails, and video "meetings" on the weekend. When Isabella questioned Jordan, the answer was always the same. "It's about work." Through the wonders of technology they were connected 24/7. Click.

Looking back on Jordan, it is easy to see the red flags that he either missed or ignored. Landing the new account was great. No problem there. Not leaning into his marriage when he knew they were drifting apart was a big red flag he missed. Failing to set boundaries was a big step in the wrong direction. He could have set up safeguards so that he and this woman were never alone together, but he did not. In fact, he did just the opposite because it felt good to be alone with her. The first emails and messages that turned personal were other ignored red flags, and then lying to Isabella was a big blow. At the end of the six weeks, Jordan had a big payout. He also was in a relationship mess that could literally cost him everything. It all started with a click.

## BLAME?

As you read these stories, my guess is that you could add one or two. Most of us know a story of infidelity that either began or grew online. So whose fault is it? Is it the internet and all the access points it affords us? No. The responsibility is still ours. Kevin made the choice to pursue an old girlfriend. Quinn put her profile on a dating site. Jordan fostered a working relationship and turned it in a different direction. The responsibility is ours. It's telling ourselves no. It's praying for strength. It's not crossing those lines that we know we should not cross. It's clicking on the things that are good and healthy for us and not clicking on the others.

The choices you make and the temptations you face are greatly framed by the way you view the computer in front of you, the gateway it is to the internet, and all the ways of connecting with others who are a click away.

How you view it and where you let it take you are your choices. There are good roads and bad roads. Choosing the good roads will protect your marriage. Putting safeguards in place to protect you from the bad roads is a great idea. We all have our weaknesses. Being honest and doing something about them is a big step in the right direction. We all see the statistics of how the internet is killing marriages and how many affairs either begin or develop online. I want to start keeping new statistics, and I want you to be in this group: it's for the people who don't click. I want a community that is bound together by honoring God, themselves, their spouse, and their marriages online day in and day out. I want something we can all celebrate together. Are you in?

US

I remember the Christmas that I surprised my family with our very first computer. I was so excited and could hardly wait for all of them to see it under our tree on Christmas morning. Everyone gathered around as I plugged it in.

Before I tell you what happened, let me give you a little background. This computer was not made by Apple. It was made by a local company that was flourishing at the time. I felt lucky to get one. I remember picking it up a few days before Christmas and the guy at the store asking me if I had any questions. I said, "Nope." I knew I could read the manual and figure it out myself. Actually setting aside time to study the manual before Christmas though? That never happened. Now, back to our living room floor on Christmas morning. I plugged the monitor into the computer and the computer cord into the wall. Flipping the "On" switch, I could not wait to see the things I had seen on the demo computers at the store. This is what we saw. A dark screen that probably measured nine by nine inches with a flashing green cursor. That was it. I clicked every key on the keyboard and always got the same result. The air quickly went out of my Christmas present balloon. I had no idea how to make the computer do anything.

Over the next few years, things in the computer world changed rapidly and became very user friendly. In 1985, a company called AOL entered our lives. We had a way to connect to the internet. Over the next decade or so, the internet became a part of our everyday lives. It was very slow compared to today, but we were amazed at all it could do.

When we look at life with the internet, so much has transpired in the last twenty years. Changes and advances happened so quickly that staying up to date is a daunting task. Both the good and the bad things about the internet have grown up side by side. That's where we came in. We had to decide how we were going to deal with this new presence in our lives. It was then, and still is now, a work in progress for us. How do we embrace and use the good and shut out the bad?

Here are some things to think about:

- What filters do you need on your computer? When making this decision, think about who has access to it in your home.
- How will you monitor your kids' internet access and time online?
- As husband and wife, how can you be completely open and transparent with each other as to internet use?
- What are ways to use the internet for good?
- How can you grow your marriage through the internet?
- How can you protect your marriage through the internet?
- Who will each of you be accountable to with your internet usage?

## FINAL THOUGHTS

The internet is not going away. If you are not proactive in setting guidelines and boundaries with the internet in your home, with each other, and with your family, you will encounter the bad side. This is one of the easiest things to put off and say, "We will do it later." Later needs to be now. Later has really, really bad consequences.


## KEYS TO HANDLING THE INTERNET

As we complete this chapter, here are some things I want you to think about:

- What are some positive ways you can use the internet for good in your marriage?
- Make a "no click" list together of online places neither of you will go.
- Where are you vulnerable online? What are you doing or can you do to protect yourself and your marriage?

---

### Going Deeper

Spend some time together online looking for opportunities to grow your marriage. It could be a new book to read together. It could be a podcast to listen to or a video to watch together on growing your marriage. You could search for marriage classes or retreats to attend in your area. The internet is a great marriage tool. Don't miss out on the opportunities it gives you.

---

# EPILOGUE

That was quite a ride. Over the course of these 14 Keys, I hope you were challenged and encouraged. I know for many of us there are things to work on both individually and as a couple. Some of you may feel lost. You may be asking, "Where do I start?" If that is you, start with God. He knows where you are and everything you are dealing with. He also has the answers. Next, find a good Christian counselor. That way you have someone to walk with you, pray for and with you, and guide you to the path of healing. There is great hope for you and your marriage. I have seen God's miracles in lives and marriages over and over again. You can trust Him. He will never let you down and will always do what is best for you.

For others of you, getting started will look like revisiting all the chapters. Highlight what especially spoke to you and what you would like to spend more time working on. Then put them in order of priority for your marriage. Now you have your starting place at the top of your list. Go back through each chapter and look at the opportunities for engagement. Then look at the "Keys" and "Going Deeper" sections. Take your time working through the chapter. Stay on track and don't rush through it. Pray for God's wisdom, guidance, and healing. Go through the same process with each chapter you highlighted.

I know for many of us this book is not an easy read. It was not meant to be. The goal is to not just finish the book, but to change your marriage. I want you to grow in commonality, empathy, personal health and friendship, talking, intimacy, and sex. Let those become permanent fixtures in your marriage.

I want you to heal and grow in the rough areas that affect you and your marriage. Be the best parents possible, but don't put your marriage on hold for your kids. If addiction is a part of your marriage, deal with it now and surround yourselves with all the help available. If you have wrongly framed your spouse as your enemy, I want you to take the time to reframe your spouse. Look at money pitfalls and let God help you change where change is needed. If there is distance between the two of you, whether physical or emotional, start closing the gaps. Take time to look at your family of origin and the role models you were around. Take the good forward and leave the bad behind. Finally, be honest with each other about the internet and fix the areas that need to be fixed.

Thank you for taking the time to read this book. I pray that God will use it to give you the marriage He dreamed of just for you.

# ACKNOWLEDGMENTS

Thanks to my amazing agent Greg Johnson, who had the vision for this book.

To Keren Baltzer and Grace Johnson and all the people at FaithWords who believed in this project, I am very thankful. It has been a joy to work with you.

My Awesome Marriage team is the very best. Christina Dodson is the absolute, hands-down, most amazing administrator ever. Nils Smith continues to amaze me as our director of innovations and a valued friend. Lindsay Few is my personal editor, and nothing goes public without her approval. Andy Knight, Megan Peverall, Martha Fisher, David Underwood, and Tiffany Miller all play important roles in the success of this ministry.

Again, I saved the best for last. Nancy gets me like no one else ever could. She is my partner in everything I do and God's greatest blessing to me in this life.

# BIBLIOGRAPHY

*Cambridge Dictionary.* American English. "Internet." Accessed March 1, 2018. https://dictionary.cambridge.org/us/dictionary/english/internet.

Degges-White, Suzanne, "The 13 Essential Traits of Good Friends." *Lifetime Connections* (blog). *Psychology Today.* Posted March 23, 2015. Accessed February 6, 2018. https://www.psychologytoday.com/blog/lifetime-connections/201503/the-13-essential-traits-good-friends.

Engs, Ruth C. "What Are Addictive Behaviors?" Indiana University Bloomington, Alcohol Research and Health History. Adapted from *Alcohol and Other Drugs: Self-Responsibility.*, Bloomington, IN: Tichenor Publishing Company, 1987. http://www.indiana.edu/~engs/hints/addictiveb.html.

Google Dictionary. "Intimacy." Accessed February 22, 2018. https://www.google.com/searchq=intimacy+definition&oq=intimacy+de&aqs=chrome.0.0j69i57j0l4.3068j1j4&sourceid=chrome&ie=UTF-8.

Jamieson, Bobby. "A Deeper Look at What the Bible Says about Money." Explore God. Accessed February 7, 2018. https://www.exploregod.com/what-the-bible-says-about-money-paper.

National Heart, Lung, and Blood Institute. "Why Is Sleep Important?" Accessed February 12, 2018. https://www.nhlbi.nih.gov/node/4605.

*Oxford Living Dictionaries.* English. "Mammon." Accessed February 5, 2018. https://en.oxforddictionaries.com/definition/mammon.

Vasel, Kathryn. "6 in 10 Americans Don't Have $500 in Savings." January 12, 2017. CNN Money. Accessed February 5, 2018. http://money.cnn.com/2017/01/12/pf/americans-lack-of-savings/index.html.

# ABOUT THE AUTHOR

Dr. Kim Kimberling has been a professional counselor for over thirty years. He holds a PhD and a Doctor of Ministry in Christian Counseling. He also holds master's degrees in Christian ministry and theological studies. Dr. Kim is president and co-founder of Awesome Marriage, which reaches thousands of people with God's plan for marriage and relationships. Dr. Kim's inspiration and passion for marriage began at a young age as he watched his parents live out the true meaning of having an Awesome Marriage centered on God's incredible plan. He is open and honest about the struggles he has experienced in his own marriage and uses these personal examples to help others. He lives with Nancy, his wife of over forty years, in Oklahoma City, Oklahoma.

# GROW *Your Marriage* PURPOSEFULLY *Each Day*

Marriage is hard and life is busy. Which is why we need real, practical reminders of ways to build an awesome marriage.

Sign up for the daily One Thing email, and Dr. Kim will send you one practical thing you can do to improve your marriage that day.

 SUBSCRIBE TO DR. KIM'S **ONE THING** EMAIL AT: **WWW.ONETHING.EMAIL**

## BUILD *an* AWESOME *Marriage*

# AWESOME MARRIAGE PODCAST

Too many marriages today are struggling to survive when God intended for them to thrive. Be intentional about strengthening your marriage by tuning into the **Awesome Marriage Podcast.** On the podcast we have honest conversations about marriage and share practical advice on how to have a God-honoring, awesome marriage.

Subscribe to the **Awesome Marriage Podcast** on **iTunes or Google Play.**

Visit **www.awesomemarriage.com/podcast** to find episode notes, extra resources, and more.